Where the Dirt Road Leads

Mandy Owen

Where the Dirt Road Leads

8 Owls Publishing creates books that effectively advance God's Kingdom. You may find the full list of the books we offer on our website at 8owlspublishing.com.

Cover and Interior Design: 8 Owls Publishing

Please note that 8 Owls Publishing uses capitalization when referencing God and/or other Kingdom terminology that may differ from other publishers or grammatical trends. 8 Owls Publishing uses the English Standard Version of the Bible, published by Crossway in Wheaton, Illinois, unless otherwise noted.

ESV: Study Bible: English Standard Version. Wheaton, Ill: Crossway Bibles, 2007. Print.

ISBN: 978-1-952618-00-0

This book is dedicated to my family who stood by me when I pushed them away. Who fought for me when I was weak. Who picked me up when I was broken. Who unconditionally loved me. Thank you for never giving up and loving me through it all.

Marc, my love.
Caitlyn, my warrior.
Caylee, my wise soul.
Jovie, my joyful spirit.
Christy, my sounding board.
Dad, my rock.
Judy, my never-ending supporter.
Mom, my caregiver in times of need.

CONTENTS

Foreword

This book is written for those who truly love the Lord Jesus Christ. However, somewhere along the journey of life, you lost track of the road that leads home to Him. The issues of life, past mistakes, dehumanizing abuse, and deep pain may all play a part in causing us to lose sight of our first love–Jesus.

If you're like me, as a child I loved God with my entire soul. My deep love for Him unfortunately targeted me for the enemy's schemes. From an early age, those schemes included woundedness and abuse, which later in life fueled a deep sense of rejection and poor choices. I can't blame all my problems on Satan, but he was certainly a catalyst in the devastation of my early years–before I became known as Mighty.

This book is my story of life, love, rejection, pain, mistakes, and thankfully, overcoming. It is a road map of how I changed my stars to align with Jesus Christ. In doing so, He brought joy and fulfillment to this once broken vessel.

I recently heard a teaching that stated the road to righteousness starts when 51% or more of your heart is wanting to do the right thing. How many of us, at some point in our lives, have fallen into a pit–wanting so badly to do the right thing? But instead, we continue to make mistake after mistake to the point that we feel completely lost and unforgivable. You are not alone. We all make mistakes. Some are so bad and dirty we shy away from telling anyone what we did or how we lived. During the darkest, dirtiest stages of my life, I still loved the Lord and my heart wanted to do right more than it wanted to do wrong. So, in some sense, I guess you could say I was on the path of righteousness even when I was running away from God–making mistake after mistake. This is my story of how Jesus led me back onto that road to righteousness. I pray the Lord uses it as a roadmap for any who are stumbling off the path. Lord, I pray that You make known to everyone reading this book Your path of life, joy, and pleasures forevermore.

Psalm 16:10-11

"For you will not abandon my soul to the dead or let your holy one see corruption. You make known to me the path of life; in your presence there is fullness of joy; at Your right-hand pleasures forevermore."

Chapter One
Lost Innocence

Mighty, mighty–Mighty Mandy Mo! I can remember hearing my sweet Aunt Debbie sing this rhyme to me as a toddler while I laughed at the love I felt through her song. Although I didn't understand then, my Aunt Debbie was prophetically singing over me the truth of who I would eventually become. God knew that one day I would be mighty in His eyes. That distant day wouldn't come until my initials changed from MM to MO. I'm not trying to be confusing. It's just when she sang this over my life, my name was Mandy Maston (MM). Thirty-four years later, at the age of thirty-seven, I became Mandy Owen (MO). The first thirty-four years of my life were an absolute struggle, but it is what made me a survivor and a mighty warrior today.

I came from a very loving and stable family. My father, mother, and stepmother have all been ruthlessly devoted to me since day one. My sister and I have seen each other through every life event–good and bad. She became the one person in my life in whom I truly shared everything. However, just because you have a loving and devoted family, doesn't ensure you will have a life full of happiness.

We all face a real spiritual enemy that comes to rob, kill, and destroy. Satan tried taking me out more than once.

My mom shared with me many times that she saw a calling on my life from a young age. I remember her asking me to lay hands on her and pray for her headaches to go away. People would come to our house, and she would ask me to pray for them. I was young, but I loved the Lord–and I loved to pray. I don't ever remember not loving Jesus. He has just always been a part of my life. I know we all must decide to follow Jesus, but I must have made that decision when I was small. My mom said that when I prayed, things would happen. God would answer my prayers. Now I don't really remember all of this, but I do know my mom believes it. Maybe Satan believed it too because life events started happening that were out of my control. There certainly is something to be said about the faith of a child.

With that in mind, let me share with you the truth of my painful story.

Satan's attack on my Kingdom identity started while I was a small child. I was molested by my grandfather. It lasted years. Even after the molestation began, I chose to go to my grandfather's house to visit. He would give me gifts and tell me how much he loved me. Honestly, I felt special and loved by him. I desired the affection he gave me because that is a normal desire of every four-year-old little girl. However, I began to learn that those desires led to harm. I remember him touching me while I prayed to God to make it stop. However, I would still go back to his house. I kept our secret like he asked because I felt as though it was his way of showing that he loved me.

Even as a small child, I knew this behavior wasn't right. It brought much confusion into my soul. How could I be so hurt, but also feel so special? This pattern would follow me for many years. I felt tremendous guilt over the fact that I enjoyed his affection, but I kept it all a secret.

Deep-down, I felt as though his attention (that I didn't like) must be caused by something I was doing. *It must have been my fault.*

The trauma continued when I got a little older. I was out of school and decided to spend the day with my stepdad at his job site. He owned a construction company specifying in contract painting. The job site was in a new housing development in a remote wooded area. This made it easy for one of his helpers to rape me in the woods behind the job site. I can remember how painful it was and how dirty I felt. After it was over, I sat in my stepfather's truck with the windows rolled up in the heat of the day. I sat there all day, too ashamed to move until he could drive me home. We drove home in silence. My mom could see something was wrong, but she wasn't sure what it was.

Inside I was screaming, "Please figure this out and help me!" But externally, I never said a word. *Now I was certain it was all my fault.*

I was convinced that I must have caused these things to happen. The lie that was being fed to me was that a normal desire for love and affection must be the cause of these horrific experiences.

I know now that there is no way a child can be responsible for the perverted mind of a grown man. I also know now that none of their actions were my fault. The truth is that desiring to be loved is a human need in which predators use to manipulate their victims. I believe that my grandfather primed me for the other abusers in my life. Had I not been damaged at an early age I might have known how to protect myself.

As it was, I did not know how to use my voice.

This cycle did not stop in my childhood. You see, I have told you about the abusers in my early years, but my real abuser–the one who changed my life forever–would not come until I was older.

Eventually, somewhere around the age of eight or nine, the pain inside me grew too big. I told my sister Christy about what was happening with my grandfather. I can remember that conversation being one of the most difficult moments I have ever had in my life. The boldness and strength it took was almost too much. This is why so many children stay silent. A study by an organization called *Think You Know* states that one in three sexually abused children do not tell anyone at the time of the trauma. The top three reasons for not telling are:

> *1. They feel ashamed or embarrassed.*
>
> *2. They are not sure how to talk about it; or can't find the space.*
>
> *3. They are worried about how other people will respond and the repercussions that follow.*

For me, I felt all of the above. When I was ready to tell, I lacked the proper vocabulary needed to have the appropriate conversation. I tried to explain what was taking place but couldn't find the right words that didn't make me feel completely humiliated. Eventually, I was able to get enough out that my sister began to understand what I was trying to say. She adamantly encouraged me that my only course of action was to tell our dad.

Now I want to stop here for a moment. Had my sister not forced me to tell our dad, I never would have. The abuse would have continued and who knows where I would have ended up. Know that when a child comes to you, telling you something that is important to them, please listen! Don't brush it off and sweep it under the rug. You may be the one person able to save them from a life of abuse. My sister all but forced me to tell our dad. At the time, I hated her for it because I didn't want to have to go through telling that story again. It was humiliating; and again, I felt like it was my fault. However, she wanted to protect me, and I will forever be grateful to have her as my sister and for the bold stand she took with me.

That conversation with my dad was nearly impossible. But what was worse, was the look of sadness on his face when he realized what I was saying. I will say that what happened next was a catalyst to my healing years later when all the emotional damage from this abuse started surfacing. My dad confronted his own father. Of course, my grandfather lied and said that if I misunderstood his affections that he was sorry. My dad had a choice in that moment to either believe the whitewash from my grandfather, or to stand by me.

He chose me.
He chose not to shove me in a corner.
He chose not to strengthen the message that I wasn't important or that I must have imagined something.

No! Even though he may have struggled with those thoughts due to my age, he never said that to me. At the time, my dad was not an overly loving man. He never really hugged us, or even said, "I love you," until we were much older. However, what he did that day screamed, "I love you!" from the rooftops. This would echo in my ears the rest of my life.

In confronting my grandfather, my dad walked next door to their house while I hid in my room. I remember being so afraid of what was happening. Of course, the confrontation upset several other family members. My dad never told me exactly what was said or what happened. I just know that the rest of the family supported my grandfather while my eight or nine-year-old damaged self, sat crying in my room. I also remember how angry my dad was when he returned from my grandparent's house. He told me we would not be going back to visit. My father decided to separate from his family and chose me instead. *He was truly my hero.*

I knew from that day forward that he would always have my back, no matter what. No one from my dad's family ever talked to me about what happened. It was just swept under the rug and forgotten. I have never been able to understand how nobody cared enough to talk to me, but I never asked them either. It was just left under the rug like an underlying demon working to destroy the family. My dad is your typical fixer. That's how he showed love. If we had a problem, he fixed it. So consequently, that's how he dealt with this situation with his family.

He fixed it; and now it was fixed.
That's it.
Now let's move on.

My dad acted decisively, but he didn't know how to talk to me about what happened or how to help me. I am not sure it was even on his radar to need to do anything else.

For me, I was simply happy that he stopped it from happening. I didn't want to hurt him by talking about it again. It would be five years later, when I hit adolescence and seemingly lost my mind, that we would approach the subject. At that point, we were forced to address some of my emotional issues. About age thirteen, I became incredibly angry at the world, but didn't understand why I was so angry all the time. What my thirteen-year-old brain didn't grasp was that all the internal damage I received as a child was surfacing and showing itself in behavioral problems.

It is important to know that after I told my dad, I never told anyone else about what happened. My parents divorced when I was about four, and when all this came out, I was at my dad's house for the summer. Telling my dad was the hardest thing I had done up until that moment and I was not about to go through that again by telling my mom. Therefore, my mom did not know what had happened. She and my dad didn't speak of it.

When I hit my troubled adolescent stage, I was living with my mom, and she had no idea what was wrong with me. All she knew was that I was not myself. She was afraid that she was losing me. I remember going to Florida for a family vacation. The rest of the family was dressed in shorts and bright, fun colors. I was all "gothed" out in black. I am sure that I stood out like a sore thumb and that my mother was worried to death.

I remember being asleep one morning and my mom entering my room. She began to pray over me. I believe she anointed me with oil. I know she woke me up praying in the Spirit. I became angry and yelled at her to leave me alone. But I'm certain that she reached Jesus that day in prayer. It was something I never forgot because, even though I was angry at her for waking me up, she loved me enough to pray for me. To this day, I see hurting people who are angry and wonder if anyone is praying for them. We always hear the saying, "Hurt people–hurt people." But truthfully, freed people must pray for the hurting to be freed.

So many hurting kids don't have moms who pray for them. I was blessed with a Granny who taught both my mom and me how to pray. My mom did not always go to church, but she believed–and my Granny imparted to her the understanding of the power of prayer. She knew that prayer was powerful because my Granny had proven it to her through her own life examples and struggles.

My mom in turn showed me on several occasions how to fast and pray when situations turned bad. One time, my mom fasted for so many days I thought she was going to get sick. We needed a house and she decided to "pray it through" until it happened. She was a living example to me on how to pray which became foundational in my adult life. This taught me to anoint my own children with oil and pray over them while sleeping when I knew they were going through something tough situations.

Because my mom needed answers about my emotional state, I eventually told her what had happened with my grandfather. She was devastated. She went into her room and slept for about a week. I didn't understand why she locked herself away from me. Again, I felt like I did something wrong. *It was my fault she was hurting.*

I would learn after having my own kids that during this time she was aching inside, and it was the only way she could cope. After she emerged from her initial despair, she went into repair mode. You see, my dad had fixed the problem from happening again, but my mom now needed to help me repair the damage it left.

She sent me to counseling, and from there, the choice was made to put me in a behavioral hospital. Back in the late 1980's and early 1990's, hospitals like these where well-funded. They actually had a fantastic 24/7 therapy program. I would be leery of what happens in those hospitals today. They tend to staff "cyber" doctors and have extraordinarily little funding. If you don't have the money for a private institution, few good options are available. However, l was lucky enough, even though I didn't realize it at the time, to have this intensely personal therapy. I entered treatment hating my mom for putting me there, but I came out loving her for caring enough about me to seek help.

While inside, I met my match in an amazing tech named Larry. He was a big, burly man with a full beard in his forties. He didn't take my crap! He was the one person who, for the first time, really understood me. He told me before I left that he and I may not be from the same breed of horse, but we came from the same coral.

He spoke my language.

After he broke through my attitude, he helped me let go of the hurt I had been feeling. During those thirty days, I was cracked open like an egg, and all the goo that was built up inside was released. I can't say that it was "one-stop, fix-all, program," but it did open me up and start the process. I also realized that I didn't feel alone anymore.

Another pretty cool thing happened while I was in the hospital. My paternal grandmother sent me a gift. It was a green and white striped shirt with a white collar. Anyone who lived in the 1990's probably remembers that shirt. I loved it. She did not call or talk to me, but she sent me a peace offering to let me know she loved me. Up until this moment, I thought she hated me. But truthfully, she just didn't know what to say. She did love me, and so did my uncle–my dad's brother. My uncle ended up being a staple in my adult life. "Unky," as I call him, became a person I hold dear to this day. And in this season, my teenage life improved dramatically.

It was the beginning of my healing.

In the first chapter of my life, I had no choice over the hand of cards in which I was dealt. It was a hand that was given to me. I was powerless to control the things that happened. It is in this state of powerlessness where Satan tries to take out key players in the Kingdom. He knows that in many cases these players are unguarded and unnoticed. It is vitally important for schoolteachers, Sunday school teachers, children's church workers, counselors, and everyone charged with caring for children, to listen and pay attention to what they are saying. You may be the person God placed in that child's life to give them hope for tomorrow.

Those who feel powerless need to know this: God will never leave you, nor forsake you. He is with you in your pain and will use everything you have gone through for good, if you surrender it all to Him.

The scars from this season of my life have no ill effect on me anymore. I am left only with love and compassion for abusers who are tormented by their patterns; abuse victims who feel lost and damaged, and in many cases angry; and family members who have been left holding broken pieces for so long they don't know how to put them back together.

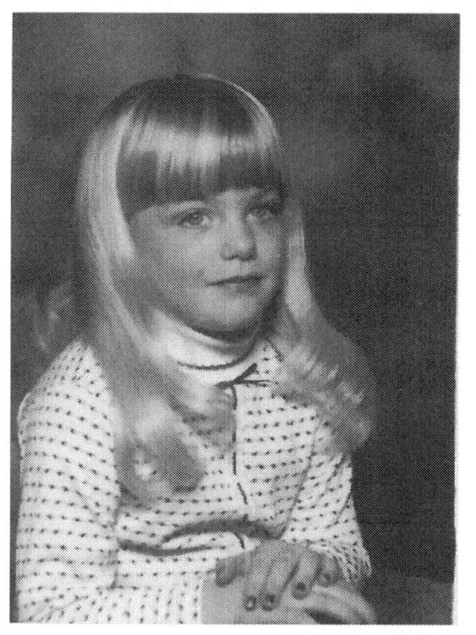

Beginnings

Snow day with my dad

On vacation with my dad and stepmom

My mom, Christy, and me

Me, dad, and my sister Christy
(Christmas, early 1980's)

Chapter Two

Intersections

It is certainly true that seasons change. Mercifully, God gives us the people, the tools, and the places we need to help us heal and move forward. I needed friends who understood and accepted me. Jonathan Malone and Angela Wroble were those friends. I had met them before my mom intervened and sent me to the behavioral hospital. God would bring both friends in and out of my life during different seasons. But the impact they had on me brought hope and the genuine connection I needed.

I remember meeting Jonathan when I was in 8th grade. I was still "gothed" out, and he was in his Buddy Holly phase. He said that he was afraid of me because I walked around with what he described as an angry chip on my shoulder. According to Jonathan, I seemed to be angry with the world at large. We didn't hit it off at first.

Just so you know, that "angry at the world chip on my shoulder" was a mask I wore to keep people at a distance. I had learned that people hurt you and I was tired of being hurt.

I then met Angela Wroble in front of the vending machine at Red Oak High School my freshman year. She turned out to be a kindred spirit whom I shared everything with throughout high school. She has been a tremendous support throughout my life. Angela was this beautiful, thin Italian girl–one of the most gorgeous girls I have ever met. We had this immediate emotional connection because of so many personal similarities in our lives. We completely understood each other. She taught me a multitude of life principles.

One of the most important lessons I learned from that friendship is that we are all screwed up–even the pretty people! When I looked at her, I thought she was perfect. I was chunky and I felt like the ugliest girl in the room (which is so not true looking back, but I certainly remember that feeling). One night, with tears in her eyes, she told me she wished she had curves like me. I thought, *"WHAAAT? Are you crazy? You are perfect! Why would you want anything I have to offer?"* It boggled my mind.

To her, even though she was thin with beautiful bold Italian features, she felt inadequate. I realized at that moment that none of us think we are perfect. We all have flaws at which Satan pokes and prods to try and convince us we are less than others.

At the age of fifteen, I had a renewed outlook on life. I started a new school–The Masters Academy. This was a private school with only six kids in my graduating class. Mrs. Wyrick, the founder of the school, focused on helping those with learning disabilities and dyslexia–which I do have. Many of us at Master's thought we were there because we didn't fit in with the mainstream pretty people. We joked that it was a school for rejects. In all honesty, maybe we were a motley crew of rejects, but it was my fresh start, and I relished in it.

Guess who I ran into at Master's Academy? –Jonathan Malone. He had grown out of his Buddy Holly phase. *Well, sort of.*

Jonathan was, and still is, one of those guys everyone knows and loves. A big goofy nut who walks on the silly side of life, but in the coolest way possible. He cracks jokes and finds humor in the most inappropriate situations, but that's just Jonathan's way.

Jonathan moved in and out of my life at various stages, but later, he would become a constant presence. He is one of those people who I always trust and can count on–no matter what. Back then, he was a true friend who grew to accept me and love me with all my flaws. He became one of my best friends in high school, as well as later in my adult life. He is someone I couldn't imagine doing without in life.

Have you ever heard the phrase *"They are my person?"* Jonathan fits the bill, and I don't have many.

I also met Amber Linker who was important to me in many ways. Again, she accepted me and was my friend when I needed one. God knows how to put people in our lives that help us connect the dots. Amber was certainly that. It was my friendship with her that led me to her family's church. The Linker's, and their church named House of Praise were game changers for my family. This began the Master's Academy phase of life.

Looking back, it is easy to see God connecting the dots for me through the people he brought into my life. He placed people around me that would steer me toward Him when needed. Of course, the enemy did the same. His negative influencers were also placed around me. It is important to pay attention to the people who support you and speak truth into your life. Sometimes it is easier to run with the friends who make life easier. But the truth speakers–you hold on to those!

I started dating a boy whom I fell in love with my sophomore year. I honestly thought I was going to marry him. We were inseparable. I thought he was perfect except he had a slight lying problem which would eventually cause our breakup my junior year. He was not a truth speaker, and I eventually saw the situation for what it was and moved on.

However, during our relationship, he invited me to visit a church he wanted to try. Neither of us had been there before, but since he wanted to go, I went with him. We arrived a bit early and sat on the far side of the small sanctuary. It was more of a large room with two aisles, but I remember we sat on the far-right side.

As I sat engulfed in conversation with my boyfriend, I looked up to see my paternal grandparents coming down the aisle. My stomach dropped and I began to panic. It had been years since we had spoken. My thoughts raced inside my head, "What am I supposed to do? My grandmother doesn't hate me because she sent me that shirt. But what do I say? Do I ignore them and sit through service? Do we leave? No, I can't leave. I will have to stand up in the middle of the service and walk right past them to sneak out of the tiny room."

The walls seemed to get smaller. I think I started to hyper-ventilate. My boyfriend begged for us to leave. Finally, I got a handle on myself. I decided to sit through the service and sneak out at the end. I honestly don't have a clue about what was preached during that service. The entire time my mind was fixated on exiting that building before the walls began to cave in on me.

Finally, the service finished. I struggled with the thought of just leaving without saying, "Hello" to my grandmother. *"I just can't do that! Or can I?"*

I squeaked out a prayer, *"Oh Jesus, I need your help! Please give me strength to get through this."*

I slowly walked towards the exit, praying for them to leave before I got close. That didn't happen. I noticed my grandmother looking at me. She was watching to see what my next move would be. We made eye contact, and I knew I would have to go talk to her. It had not been her fault and I loved her, but what should I say?

I finally went in for the approach, “Hello.” My grandmother started to cry and hugged me until she almost squeezed the air out of me. Then I started crying. I told my grandmother how sorry I was that it had been so long since we spoke. And, that I loved her. My grandfather hugged me, and told me he loved me, which I tried to reciprocate politely. Then we left. Just like that, it was over. The day I dreaded was over.

Since the ice had been broken, I asked my dad if he wanted to go to Christmas at Grandma and Pop’s that year. We had missed the last several Christmases and it just didn’t seem fair to punish my dad and grandmother over my grandfather’s behavior. My dad left that decision to me. I let him know that I wanted to go. But although my grandmother was thrilled, and that Christmas we reconnected, it never felt the same. I felt out of place.

Looking back, I guess it was awkward for the entire family, including my aunt and uncle. I wanted to find complete healing, but I still had a long way to go. At least now, I wouldn't hinder my dad from connecting to his family again.

My senior year prom was fast approaching, and I didn't have a date. Jonathan and I ended up going with each other, along with a group of friends. It turned out to be a great night of friendship and fun. Boyfriends come and go, but the memories you make with your true friends last a lifetime. High School graduation came. Jonathan and I recited a poem and performed a musical duet together. We walked the graduation aisle, and just like that, high school was over. We lost touch. It was now time to grow up and figure out what to do next.

As a teen, I began attending Oak Cliff Assembly and was incredibly involved with their youth group. I can't say I had close friends, but I loved the youth pastor. I learned so much from him during that season. I genuinely believe that having Pastor Scott Wilson as a youth pastor helped build the foundation for my Christian life. He modeled how to pray, teach, study, and live in a way that few pastors can. Again, God was connecting the dots for me through His people. Healing is a process, and God knows how to reveal life and truth so that we might truly be free.

In all honesty, I felt lost on what my next move should be. I decided to join a leadership/discipleship program my church had recently rolled out called Master's Commission. This was a one-year discipleship program in which we lived with church members who opened their homes. One hundred percent of our time was to be devoted to bible study, prayer, outreach, and leadership training. During this year, I was given the chance to travel to other churches and minister to families in a way I had never done before.

I learned how to lay hands on people and see them healed.
I prophesied over people with confidence.
I memorized over four hundred scripture verses.

(That I still know).

But, most of all, I learned how to talk to Jesus in an authentic way.

We were required to go to prayer every day for an hour or more, especially on youth night. We would come together in a small room and pray over the service. Although I recall many times falling asleep during this prayer hour, Pastor Scott would pace back and forth modeling to us effective prayer. Sometimes, he would scream, yell, laugh, and lay face-down sobbing, or sometimes he would sit quietly in a corner. As I watched Pastor Scott pray, he taught me how to effectively battle in prayer.

Everyone in our group seemed so close to God. Most knew they had a calling on their lives. Some were called to be preachers, some evangelists, some pastors wives, but it felt as though they had all heard from God–except me. I was still waiting on God to tell me my purpose in life. I felt an intense expectation that God was going to use me in a huge way, but I didn't know what that looked like. I desperately wanted to hear from Him. I had been saved at an early age. I was baptized twice just in case the first one didn't take. This happened in the church I visited during my childhood. I had been filled with the Holy Spirit, and trust me, that was an experience. If I can diverge from the narrative for a moment, I will tell you that story.

When I was around ten or eleven-years-old, an evangelist came to our church. He was a large man with a big scruffy beard like those worn in the 1980's. I was sitting on the back row with the other kids, and he called up anyone who wanted to receive this gift from the Lord. Well, I knew I loved Jesus, and if He had a gift to give, I wanted it. I walked up to the altar and stood there with my eyes closed waiting to receive. All the sudden, these large hands slapped me on my forehead. The evangelist had grabbed my head, and started shaking me all around, screaming, "Make love to Jesus!" Now, I am all about loving me some Jesus, but for a ten-year-old girl who had been abused and raped, this was a disgusting thought.

He kept shaking me. I could tell that he wasn't going to stop until I got this gift he mentioned. However, I couldn't get the thought of making love to Jesus out of my mind. I started praying, "God, please give me what this man wants me to have so he will stop praying for me!" And graciously, God did. I was filled with the Holy Spirit with the evidence of speaking in tongues right then.

Just so you know, the gift of the Holy Spirit is for all believers. All you must do is ask with an open heart. I sincerely asked God because I knew the gift was real. But the catalyst for me receiving the Holy Spirit in that moment was the fact that the evangelist was scaring me badly, I wanted him to leave me alone. I wish I could remember his name today. I would look him up and thank him. Just know, if you are not filled with the Holy Spirit, don't be afraid to ask God to fill you right now. He hears your prayers and wants to empower you to live for Him.

Going back to my original story, I had done everything God told me to do at the Master's Commission, but I still did not hear Him speak to me about my purpose. Not only could I not hear God about my calling, but His voice also seemed dead silent. As if I needed to ask the question, "God are you even there?"

One morning, I headed to chapel. Pastor Scott was teaching. I can still remember the topic. He taught on purpose and destiny. He said that some are called to be the leader of tens; some are called to be a leader of hundreds; some thousands; and still others a leader of millions. The question we needed to ask was, "Which leader am I?"

So, I asked,

"Which one am I?"

"What is my destiny?"

"What is my purpose?"

"God, do you want to use me?"

"God, please can you hear me?"

"Do you even want me?"

I kneeled and prayed these words to God with all my heart. I begged Him to give me an answer. "Please hear me! Please, please just want me! Please use me!" I heard nothing but dead silence. Again, I wondered, "God, are you even there?" Everyone else seemed clear on their callings. Why wasn't I? I thought, "God must not want to use me. I must not even have a purpose." My mind was telling me that wasn't true, but in the depth of my emotions, it sure did feel like it.

I finished the Master's Commission under the leadership of Mark Brewer. It was one of the best years of my life. But, towards the end, my heart just wasn't in it. I felt as though God didn't really want to use me or He would have shown me. The way I felt in my childhood resurfaced, "I am not worth much, right? Terrible things had happened to me as a kid, and I was damaged goods."

"Why would God want to use me?" I felt worthless–too damaged for God to have a calling for me. I felt unwanted. And, I had no idea where to go after the Master's Commission Graduation.

The next decision I made changed the trajectory of my life. About a month after graduation, we were to go before the Assemblies of God and be commissioned. I had found a job in the interim and I was afraid to ask off. So, I didn't go. God didn't want to use me anyway, right? That decision is one of the biggest regrets I have in my life. Who knows where I would have ended up if I had humbled myself before God during the last few months of the Master's Commission. It's possible my life would have taken a similar turn. But maybe, my path would have been much different with a lot less pain.

Poor choices began to become my pattern. I chose to believe the lie Satan fed me that the other kids in my group were better than me and more important to God. Because of that, I became bitter towards God. At the time, I never would have admitted the truth of that, but deep down it was there.

Paula was my Aunt Linda's best friend. She was a manager at a local apartment complex. After graduating the Master's Commission, I began looking for a job. I stopped in to say hello to Paula. It just so happened that she needed a leasing agent. It paid $6.50 an hour and came with a discount on an apartment. I jumped on it! This would turn out to be the beginning of my apartment industry career.

I drove a little Kia Sophia, and I needed to pay it off. This job was perfect for me. I easily made friends. They accepted me, and even liked me, unlike some of the pretty church people in which I never felt that I belonged. Let me just say, be careful not to fall into easy friendships that don't add value to your life. I am not saying friendships should be hard, but they should challenge you to be the best you possible. I realize now that not all church people are "pretty," but in my mind I felt so out of place around the kids with money, fancy cars, and lots of friends–I just called them the pretty people. Although I had no knowledge of the fact, people thought I was gorgeous. It was Paula who helped me grow in the acceptance of myself.

I moved into an apartment on the property. My sister had just gone through a divorce and needed a place to stay. She moved in with me. She liked to go to the Crystal Chandelier, the local dance hall, every Thursday night. I went along with her every once in a while. I would drink a little and my relationship with God grew distant. I could still feel His presence, but I was not walking with Him.

After about a year, I was offered a promotion. I became a roving leasing agent. This meant I was a corporate employee and would fill in at sites that needed help. Sometimes I filled in for leasing agents, assistants, or even managers. I became incredibly good at my job and proved myself to be trustworthy. One assignment was in Grand Prairie, Texas. I filled in for a manager who had been diagnosed with a serious illness and would be out for a few months.

On my first day, I met a young maintenance man on the property. He was the most handsome man I had ever laid eyes on. I went home that night and told my sister I had met the man I was going to marry.

Up until this moment, I could say I was living my life on the fence. I had not fully given my hurt over to God. I still wanted to hold onto it like a security blanket. It had become my identity. In my mind, I was who I was because of what had happened to me as a child. God wanted me to know who He created me to be and was putting people in my path to help me.

A different road had been presented to me through the Master's Commission that I could have walked down. That road probably led to ministry, happiness, and restoration. Instead, when God didn't respond to me the way I felt He should have, I pushed Him away. I wasn't going to let Him hurt me the way others had. If He didn't want me, then I would just do life by myself and forge my own path. I didn't completely walk away from God. I knew him in the depths of my soul. But emotionally, I put a wall up and separated Him from my choices. Even though the path I chose was not God's perfect will, He still had the ability to use the decisions I made for my good. I had acquired the tools I needed to survive the upcoming years.

He had given me friends that would connect me to Him when needed. Friends that loved me and spoke truth into my life. He had given me a church that taught me deep principles of the Bible. Leaders that displayed how to pray, humble themselves, and cry out to God. He had given me a job that was a major source of security for me for the next twenty years and would bring resources into His kingdom in the future.

While I was floating around trying to figure my life out, God was laying foundational stones. He has done the same thing for you. It is important, however, that we use the tools He gives us. In the upcoming chapters you will see how I needed these tools to survive. We must believe that God has given us everything we need and has planned ahead beyond our ability to ensure our success. Find the truth speakers God has placed in your life and cherish them. They will be your sounding board in the future.

Romans 8:28

"And we know that in all things God works for the good of those who love Him, who have been called according to his purpose."

Prom with Jonathan (1994)

Amber Linker and me ready for prom (1994)

Me and Angela (1990)

Please remember Master's Commission of Dallas in your prayers!

'94-'95 Master's Commission of Dallas Staff: Rev. Mark Brewer, Director; Melinda Dunkin; Rev. Shawn Lewellen

Melinda Dunkin

Melinda is from Waco, TX. She attended Southwestern Assemblies of God College for two semesters before joining MCD in 1993. She has returned a second year to join the MCD staff. She is 21 years old.

Shawn Lewellen

Shawn is from Rockford, IL. He graduated from MCD in July of 1994 and has returned a second year to serve MCD on staff. He received his credentials with the A/G in 1994. He is 22 years old.

Hector Cortes

Hector is from Mexico City, Mexico. He originally came to Dallas to work with the Spanish church based out of Oak Cliff Assembly of God. He is 28 years old.

Teresa Fluegel

Teresa came to us from First Assembly of God out of Rockford, IL. She has put her career with MGF Manufacturing on hold to be in MCD. She is 23 years old.

Chris Keating

Chris plans to attend Christ for The Nations Institute after graduating from MCD. He is from Pasadena, TX, and he is 24 years old.

Jason Kennedy

Jason is from Mesquite, and he has attended Oak Cliff Assembly for 6 years. He graduated from high school in [illegible]. He is 19 years old.

April is from Cedar Hill, TX. Her family recently moved to California, and April chose to stay in Dallas and be in Master's Commission. She is 19 years old.

Brian is from Kansas City, MO. He has attended Southwestern Assemblies of God College in Waxahachie for two years, and plans to return after graduation from MCD. He is 21 years old.

Mandy has grown up in the Dallas area, and has been part of the youth group at Oak Cliff Assembly for five years. She graduated in 1994, and she is 18 years old.

Brian joined us from Loves Park, IL, which is just outside of Rockford. He resigned his position with his father's company to come to Dallas. He graduated in 1995, and he is 19 years old.

Master's Commission Graduation

Chapter Three
A Fork in the Road

The day Shaun entered my life was the day it changed forever. Some of it was good change. Some bad. But for certain, my life would never be the same.

The first day I met him, he looked at me, but never said a word. I thought it was strange that he would not at least say, "Hi." When I tried talking to him the next day, he wrote me a note. I remember thinking, "Maybe he is sick, or has lost his voice. By the third day, my curiosity got the best of me.

Since I had not heard him speak to anyone in three days, I asked what was wrong. He wrote me a note explaining that he was on a fast for a week. He was fasting speech. Huh? Who fasts speech? I mean, sure, I had heard of fasting food, TV, and maybe even sex, but never speech.

I thought, "Wow! If he is faithful enough to fast speech for a whole week and to stick to it, he must love God. He must be a faithful man." That was it for me. He was the one. I just knew it. The connection between us was so strong, it seemed like we were meant to be together and we both felt it. We started dating. I started going to church with him at a mega church in Grand Prairie, Texas. We didn't attend this church long, but I do remember some major life lessons being taught in those sermons that stuck with me.

I learned that Shaun did everything at full speed. He was an "all there" person. However, I also quickly learned that he never finished anything he started. His passion for the Lord was present because God had truly touched his life. His encounter with God happened right before I met him which led me to believe he was a strong man of faith.

Truthfully, I didn't see how demonized he was. He soon quit going to church, and by this time, we were committed. I worked in the leasing office, and he was maintenance. He would get my attention through the "walky-talky" and sing different songs to me. I can't sing, or remember words to songs, so I would speak back the lyrics to one of my favorite movies–Grease 2:

"Who's that guy?"

"Where did he come from?"

"Who's that guy?"

Rewriting the song, I would say, *"Where can I get one?"*

He would come back with something like, "He is in unit #2105 waiting on you."

We would talk for hours. It felt as if we connected deeply and understood each other. I hadn't experienced this kind of intensity in a relationship before. Maybe what I thought was connection and understanding was just manipulation. My earlier relationships were typical boyfriends, but the depth of connection I experienced with Shaun was on a whole different playing field.

My sister was the popular one in high school. She had all the boyfriends and going into our young adult life was no different. She never lacked dates. She was beautiful and skinny. I was insecure because of my past. I always felt like I wasn't good enough, pretty enough, smart enough, skinny enough. Overall, just not enough. Shaun made me feel like I fit somewhere. He got me and it felt good.

However, one specific day, God began to whisper to me about walking away from this relationship. Shaun had missed work, and I had tried calling him all day. He didn't answer the phone. I decided to go to his apartment and check on him. I knocked, but no one answered. I could hear music inside, so I knew he was home. But again, no one answered.

I stood at the door to his apartment feeling confused as to what I was experiencing. God whispered to me and told me to leave and walk away from this relationship. Clearly, I know He told me to leave. I just couldn't make myself do it. My low self-esteem screamed for Shaun to love me. I needed to be "the one."

I had a key, so I entered his apartment. My heart was racing. Would I walk in on him with another girl? Would I make him angry by being there? I slowly turned the key, and even more slowly turned the doorknob. The door crept open as the music got louder. I peeked around the corner but didn't see anyone. I ran straight into the side bedroom before anyone could see me and hid in the bathroom. I kept trying to figure out what to say or do. I could hear a group of people in the living room, but I was too afraid to approach them. I just sat in the bathroom.

Finally, after not having the strength to confront him, I decided to sneak back out the front door and leave. I remember crying as I drove home. I didn't understand what had just happened. What was he doing in that living room that wouldn't allow him to call me or answer his phone? Why was I too scared to look? What was more important than me at that time? I didn't know, but I realized I was not capable of walking away from him. I also realized there was more to his story than I knew. He told me later that he had a few buddies over, and he was sorry he didn't call me. I never told him I was there that night. I just pretended it didn't happen.

If I had only listened to the whisper of God.

We continued to date, and eventually he asked me to move in with him. I had an apartment I shared with my sister, and I didn't want to keep putting her in a bind. I also didn't want to tell my parents that I was living with a boy. I kept my apartment but stayed with Shaun. We were inseparable.

We didn't have any real friends. He didn't like coming around my family. His family didn't have much to do with him either, so it was just us.

On a side note, this is a lesson that I learned the hard way. If someone doesn't have any deep connections with friends or family, there is usually a reason, and you should be wary. Watch how the person you're dating treats his or her parents, siblings, and friends. If they don't keep their word, or treat others well, they will not treat you well either.

Shaun had a son from a previous relationship. We would keep him at nights when his mom would go to work. I can remember one night I was asleep in the bedroom and Shaun and his son were asleep in the living room. I heard his "ex" come in to get her son, but she didn't leave. She stayed with Shaun that night in the living room. I lied to myself saying that it didn't happen, but deep down I knew the truth.

Looking back on this, I have no idea why I didn't leave then, but again, I believed I wasn't enough. I thought maybe Shaun needed someone better than me. I had convinced myself that I must be lucky that someone would even want me, right? So, I never mentioned what happened. I just ignored it. I am not sure how I arrived at this place mentally, emotionally, or spiritually. Two years before this, I was in the Masters Commission praying for God to show me my ministry. How could I love God so much, and not love myself?

Shortly after this, Shaun started showing me another side of him. He drank more than I had ever seen anyone drink before. When he got drunk, he would do drugs. He would do any kind of drugs he could find, but his favorite was crack cocaine. I guess in my young ignorance, I thought that doing drugs would be a phase–that he would have fun for a while, then he would grow up. But I was about to learn that there was a much darker side to Shaun.

God continued to whisper to me, telling me to leave. He kept warning me of what was ahead. Shaun was young. He was still trying to build his life to be the man he wanted to be. Deep down he loved me, so he would try to fight his demons. He tried to build a life for us, but he just couldn't seem to finish what he started. He would do good for about six months at a time–then just self-destruct.

I remember the first time I saw his mean streak. We had adopted this gorgeous black cat that we named Cleopatra. She was beautiful and loving, but she would stay up at night driving us crazy, then sleep during the day. One night when we were sound asleep, she wanted to play and started jumping on us.

Shaun lost it! I had never seen that kind of anger before. He jumped up, grabbed Cleopatra, and threw her out of the second story window.

I was terrified. I couldn't believe what had just happened. I couldn't sleep the rest of that night and I heard God whisper again, but this time louder, "Leave!" Again, I didn't leave. I just laid there in the quiet of the night wondering who this man was lying next to me.

We had been together for about a year when I found out I was pregnant. As confused as I was over our relationship, and as unhealthy as it had become, I believed that Shaun loved me and needed me. Looking back, I see how he tried to do the right thing for our family, but he couldn't overcome his demons. But, because of my pregnancy, he truly did try.

Our wedding day was quite simple. My dress was from the Dillard's outlet mall, and we were married in a little chapel in Irving, Texas. We had been fighting before the wedding, and I was six months pregnant. It was an emotional ordeal.

I was so happy to be having a baby, but I was only twenty-one years old. I remember the look on my family's faces when I told them I was pregnant. It was a look of disappointment. The only person who really encouraged me was my Aunt Linda. Her first response was pure joy over a new life coming into the family. I am sure underneath her joy she was thinking, "Oh boy, what is going to happen here?" But she was wise enough to know that nothing could change the future at this point. She knew encouragement was what I needed the most. I am thankful for her kind response.

I was young and felt like I had let my family down again. That precious baby girl turned out to be one of the greatest gifts God ever gave me. She would help me see my need to be pulled from darkness when I was lost and couldn't find my way out.

The day of our wedding, my best friend Angela came back to the dressing room to check on me. She could see that I was nervous. Honestly, I felt like running and never looking back; and that whisper was back. However, it wasn't quiet. It was loudly saying, "Leave, don't walk down that aisle."

Angela told me that I didn't have to do it, and that I could call the wedding off. But my family had given me so much money for this wedding. My mom, dad, and Judy all had invested money, time, and energy. I didn't feel as though I could tell them I wanted to call it off. I looked at Angela and honestly said these words, "No, my parents spent too much money. I can always divorce him later."

Seriously, what kind of messed up thinking is that? I walked down the aisle knowing that I was making the biggest mistake of my life.

The day Caitlyn was born was a joyful day. My mom and Shaun took me to the hospital, and we welcomed the most perfect baby I had ever laid eyes upon. She had a perfectly pink complexion with black hair. She was beautiful.

Shaun was there, and he fell in love with that sweet baby. All my family came and my fears of being a young mother disappeared as I looked at this precious life that would forever be ours. I knew instantly that I was meant to be her mother. I had never experienced such unconditional love. I knew I would do everything in my power to protect her. I would never let anyone, or anything, hurt her the way I had been hurt.

The years that followed were extremely hard. We had very little money, and what we did have Shaun would spend on beer or drugs. I went back to work two weeks after I delivered because we had no money for food. Shaun had quit his job again and was hoping to find something that would make him happy this time. This became his norm–always looking for something that would make him happy, but never finding it.

I don't remember where he was working when Caitlyn was born. He jumped from job to job. I do remember being severely broke.

One time, I hid my last twenty dollars in the back of my wallet so I could buy diapers. I lied to him telling him I didn't have any money, but he didn't believe me. He ransacked my purse until he found it and went to get drunk. Caitlyn was left with no diapers. I was amazed at how he could make $20.00 last all night. He had a magnetic personality and people would always cater to him. They bought him drinks and anything else he wanted. He would be out all hours of the night, while I was home alone watching the baby.

It was during this time, he started getting more manipulative and eventually abusive. It was still subtle, but a shift had occurred.

I remembered something his ex-girlfriend told me when I first started dating him. She said if a man ever hits you once, he will hit you again. I had thought it to be a strange statement, but the way she said it was like she was trying to warn me.

Oprah was at the peak of her success in those days. On her show, she voiced the thought that God gives you whispers, and if you ignore them, He will get louder and louder until finally you feel a bang! In the 1990's, she used the word God. If you google this episode now, I think she references the "universe." But I knew what she said to be true. God had been whispering to me since the beginning of my relationship with Shaun. I received several whispers that kept getting louder each time.

The physical barrier of his abusive behavior was finally broken. Shaun had been out all-night drinking and didn't come home until very early the next morning. I started a fight with him. I could see he didn't want to hear it from me, but I just couldn't keep my mouth shut. I was angry and I wanted him to know. Later that day, as we were driving, I was still arguing with him.

His eyes turned dark and scary.

He was driving, and I was in the passenger seat. Then he started pounding on my legs over and over. He just kept beating my legs like I was nothing to him. It seemed he wanted to inject the greatest amount of pain he could, but he was smart enough to not bruise a part of my body that would be seen by others.

I ended up with painful black and blue bruises up and down my legs. It hurt to walk for several days. The whispers got louder, and I began to understand why I needed to leave.

But again, I wasn't really worth anything, right? I mean this must be my fault. If I were prettier, skinnier, or a better wife he wouldn't stay out all night. If I hadn't kept arguing with him, this would not have happened, so *it must be all my fault.* Deep down, I needed this to work to prove that I wasn't a failure. I needed to know that I wasn't the cause of why all these terrible things kept happening to me.

Similar situations continued to happen throughout the next year. We eventually split up, mainly because he had given up fighting his demons. He wanted to be alone so that he could sink into his addiction without guilt or the responsibility of a family.

As I sat with Caitlyn night after night, I felt like I was the worst mother in the world. I had failed her for not making my marriage work. I had this terrible fear of her growing up alone or, that I would remarry, and they wouldn't love her the way I did. I wanted her to grow up with a full-blooded sibling. If she had that, I reasoned, no matter what happened to me, she would have someone who loved her just as strongly as I did. She had Chase, my sister's son, who had just been born. I knew they would always have each other, but I wanted another child. So, I prayed that Shaun and I would somehow work things out. My prayer was for another baby, not for my relationship with Shaun. Although things were so unstable, I knew deep in my soul I was meant to have another child.

When I became pregnant with Caylee, my marriage with Shaun was all but done. His drinking and disappearing acts were at an all-time high. I had no money. What money I did have, Shaun would take. It was 1999, and Caitlyn was a year old. We didn't have cable or smart TV's back then, so we watched VCR tapes as our choice of recreation. I mean, what else is a pregnant, broke, mother of a toddler going to do except watch the same cartoon over and over again–every single day–day after day?

Caitlyn's movie of choice was *Quest for Camelot* released in 1998. The star of this cartoon was Kayley, a young girl who was going to rescue Camelot by finding King Arthur's sword. The name Kayley stuck. On my second day at the hospital, with no name picked out for my sweet baby girl, I decided to name her after the courageous heroine from Caitlyn's favorite movie. She became Caylee Ann.

Shaun was a truck driver during the time I was pregnant with Caylee. He was gone most of the time, but he happened to be home the weekend I went into labor. I remember waking up in the middle of the night extremely uncomfortable. As I got up to go to the bathroom, I felt a gush of water and thought to myself, "Man this is an odd experience." I didn't realize at the time that my water had just broken, but I did know I didn't feel right.

I was afraid to wake-up Shaun. Instead, I waited in pain on the couch. When he got up to go to work, I told him I was hurting and really felt we needed to go to the hospital. He was busy getting ready for work and didn't want to be bothered by me. He told me I would be fine, and it would pass. He threw all his stuff in his bag and left. I remember how alone I felt. I was in pain and needed someone to be there for me.

However, I still wasn't 100% sure I was in labor, so I waited a while longer. Sitting there alone and in pain, I just cried. Finally, I called my sister who lived across the courtyard. She ran to my aide, as she always does, and helped me get into the car. Driving frantically, she said, "I have to stop for gas. I am driving on fumes!" I remember I screamed at her, "If you stop for gas, I am having this baby in your car! Just drive!"

We made it to the hospital in time to deliver, but it was a close call. My sister Christy was by my side the entire time. She held my hand and helped me push through the pain, both physical and emotional. She was the one who cut Caylee's cord.

Sometimes I remember this piece of my story with awe as Caylee and Christy are so much alike. Caylee looks more like Christy than she does me.

They have a very similar birthmark on their arm.

They both have a gap in their front teeth.

They are both introverts and use shopping as therapy (which I hate).

Their connection and similarities are amazing.

I had the privilege to be with my sister as she gave birth by cesarean to Chase. I am honored to share such a special bond by being with her as she brought him into the world. The three musketeers had entered the picture: Caitlyn, Chase, and Caylee–more siblings than cousins.

These three would do life together through the good, the bad, and the ugly. They would love each other.

Looking back, I know my sister is a God-given gift. I was heartbroken and alone when Shaun didn't care enough about me and our baby to make sure we were okay before walking out the door. But God knew that I was alone and sent someone better to my side. He not only sent me my sister (who saw me through every step of that day like a pro), He formed a much-needed bond between my sister and my daughter. It was like He said, "Okay Satan, you can try to steal the significance of this delivery, but I am stamping it with more love than baby Caylee ever knew was possible." She was perfect, and I knew from the moment I saw her that she was meant to be mine.

Shortly after Caylee was born, I noticed Shaun was completely given over to alcohol. He was gone for days at a time. When he was home, he was usually drunk. One night my mom was staying with us helping with the girls. He had been out all night. We had locked the keyless deadbolt and he couldn't get in the front door. In a drunken stupor, he screamed at us, causing a scene outside for all to see.

We were afraid to let him in. He ended up breaking out the window above Caitlyn's bed. Glass went everywhere and I was so thankful she was in my bed that night. My mom was terrified, and the kids were crying. She called the police, and he went to jail again. Life at this point had become completely dysfunctional. My marriage had become violent and unsafe. I knew my family was falling apart and needed a reprieve.

I came home from work soon after that event. Shaun had left. He had walked out on us. All his stuff was gone, and he had left without an explanation. I felt heartbroken and empty. I felt like a failure. I couldn't see the truth at the time. He needed to find someone who could support his lifestyle. He had depleted our resources and this pattern of relationship hopping was his survival mechanism.

I was deeply hurt, but honestly, it wasn't love. It was a deep desire to be loved by him and to prove my worth. I prayed and cried daily for my marriage to be restored. I found out that he had been having an affair (actually numerous affairs), but one had led to a pregnancy at the same time I was pregnant with Caylee.

There are no words to describe the feelings of abandonment and humiliation that comes when your husband leaves you for another woman and child. I had devotedly stood by him as he took me through hell. In my mind, I thought he was choosing them over us. I realized years later that he was following the resources. This woman and her child were just as much victims of his lifestyle as we were.

Regardless, at that moment all I could see was my husband and the father of my children leaving us for someone else. I snapped! I became one of those women we all make fun of for being so blind. I wrote letters to Shaun's family letting them know the truth. I would call him constantly. I would find any excuse to call him and would use the girls crying for him or being sick as an excuse to reach out. It was even more hurtful when he didn't care. I stalked him by driving around the areas I thought he might be frequenting. The only time he seemed to care was when he needed something from me, and anytime he called me, I would run to him.

Knowing me today, people would be shocked that I could be this person that I describe. I am embarrassed to even think I was that weak, but I was a broken and depressed wreck of a woman. I can't even imagine how my family saw me during this season.

Eventually Shaun's affair ended, and of course, I took him back. I mean I had been praying and begging God to restore my marriage. Why on earth did I think anything would be different? But, this time, I was determined to make this marriage work. Still internalizing everything as being my fault, I tried harder to be funnier, prettier, cook better, and accept his lifestyle. I had drifted so far from God at this point that I was wide open for Satan's schemes–and he went in for total destruction.

I thought I would party with Shaun to try to connect with him more. That was a mistake! We started down the most destructive path of drug addiction I had ever experienced. It almost destroyed me. I lost my job and started leaving my kids with my family all the time. I was lying to the people I loved and was destroying everything good in my life. I wrote hundreds of hot checks to buy more drugs. I would write a $25 hot check and have to pay a $75 fee on that check just so I could go score one more time. My life hit rock bottom.

My daughter recently told me that she remembered one weekend that I had dropped her off with family and she told them that she knew I would never come back.

One weekend, Shaun owed a drug dealer about $800. He came home and said that we needed to move that night because someone was after him. We had two small babies, pockets full of drugs, and we needed to move. We left everything of sentimental value behind–everything I had built. It was all left behind.

We packed up the necessities and left overnight. Years later, I ended up paying off the debt from that apartment. But during this season, we just moved from place to place.

It seemed like every few months we would end up moving again. There was no stability in our life. Trying to rebuild and get away from the drug scene, Shaun and I packed up the girls and moved to East Texas near my mom. We literally showed up on her doorstep after sleeping in the car all night on the side of the road with our two small babies. I am sure her husband was less than overjoyed when he saw us on his doorstep. We stayed with her a few days, but quickly found a cheap trailer that we could rent. It was horrible! Truly, the worst place I had ever lived! I was always afraid at night–afraid of something happening to us.

Shaun found a job with a trucking company and again was gone most of the time. We did okay for a couple of months, but as soon as he got his first big check, his demons came knocking on the door. He would spend all his money at the bar, or the crack house. His main addiction was alcohol. But he had no resistance to drugs when he drank.

Even though I felt far away from God, I never stopped loving Him. I can remember in the midst of my addiction praying and asking God to not "rapture" everyone out of the world that night, but to give me more time to get myself together. I knew God's ways. I realized that Shaun had become an idol in my life. Something that I worshipped. Maybe the idol was the desire I had for him to love me.

One night in that trailer, after Shaun had spent all his money and came home stone cold drunk, I saw that familiar shift in his eyes. They turned dark and something evil came over him. His eyes looked like the time in the apartment in Euless, Texas, when Shaun trapped me in the apartment after beating me. He was threatening to kill me, but making it appear to our neighbors that I was the one threatening him. He held a knife to me saying that he would kill me. I was screaming and crying. He would then speak in a loud voice saying,

"Mandy, what's wrong with you? Why are you crying? I love you! I want to help you! Please baby, don't do this! Put the knife down, please. I love you!" But at the same time, he would whisper in my ear, "I am going to kill you, and everyone will think it is self-defense."

When he would get like that, he was usually severely drunk. It was like he took on a different persona. He didn't even look like himself. He looked dark and evil.

Often, when he was like this, he would black out and wake up the next morning not remembering anything. Sometimes he would confess things from his nights out, but then he would wake up and not remember any of it. It was a hard burden to carry, knowing pieces of the secrets he carried, but not understanding everything.

He came home one night, and I knew he had done something horrific, or had hurt someone badly. He kept rambling and confessing how sorry he was, but he would never tell me the entire story. I wanted to call the police and report it, but I didn't know what to say. *"My husband came home drunk, rambling?"* If I could have gathered a few more details, I would have called the police. But all I had was a gut feeling.

That night in the cheap trailer, he went crazy. He beat me and accused me of cheating on him. He told me that he was going to kill all of us. I was trapped and couldn't leave the trailer. The girls were sleeping, and I was so afraid that he was going to hurt them. Shaun had never been physically abusive to the girls–only me. But he wasn't himself that night. I was terrified and genuinely thought we were all going to die.

He eventually got tired and was ready to pass out. But, he knew that I would leave as soon as he did. He made me get the girls and get in bed next to him. He laid right next to me and told me that if I tried to leave, he would kill us. He ended up passing smooth out. I was terrified and laid motionless for hours. I was so afraid that if I tried to crawl out of bed he would wake up and the whole ordeal would start all over again.

I laid there and prayed.

Eventually, I mustered up the courage to try to escape and I slowly crawled out of bed. I moved just a few inches and waited to see if he moved. I would move a few more until I inched my way off the bed. That is when I realized we had a chance. I grabbed the girls and ran outside.

The girls had gone through that experience on several occasions. They were both under five-years-old and had learned to be silent and still for hours lying next to me. They knew not to make daddy mad and to be as quiet as possible. At that young age, my girls had been forced to learn to be my protector, due to the fact that I could not be theirs. They knew what would happen to me if a fight broke out, and they were afraid of what could happen to them. They obeyed faithfully to keep the peace. When fights did break out, Caitlyn would take care of Caylee until it was over. They would wait for Shaun to fall asleep, then comfort me when I was crying–or hold me when I had no tears to cry. I was carrying Shaun's burdens and the girls were carrying mine.

Shaun had taken the car keys and put them in his pocket that night so he would know if I tried to leave. There was no way I was going to try and fish them out. I just wanted out of that house before we died. We rushed out the door with no car, no shoes on our feet, and no money–just our lives. The nearest phone was a few miles away down a dirt road, so we started walking. The road was rough and hurt our feet each step we took. I tried carrying the girls as much as I could. Caylee was the smallest, so I carried her almost the entire way. But, Caitlyn had to walk most of that road with me.

My biggest regret in life is that my kids had to walk down this abusive road that I traveled. Not just this road, but the entire journey. I wish I had listened to God's whispers. I wish I had spared them all of the pain.

I walked down this road knowing full well that it was my doing–my choice. Yes, Shaun was abusive, and yes, I was primed for abuse in my childhood. But, I also had tremendous family support. I had chosen the wrong path.

It was my fault, not anyone else's, that my girls had to walk that road that day–and the road full of pain they endured afterwards. However, the wonderful thing about dirt roads is you never know where they lead.

After we finally got to the phone, I realized I didn't have any money. I made a collect call to one of the only people I had left–my mom. She came and picked us up from that gas station looking a mess.

I can only imagine what she was thinking that day.

From day one of this season of my life, God whispered to me and the whispers got louder. I chose to ignore them. God didn't want me to go through the pain of abuse. He wanted me to choose Him and walk away. My stubbornness and insecurity caused me to search for something that wasn't there. I didn't get the answers from God I wanted, so I forged my own path. A path which took me off the road of righteousness and down a dirt road of destruction. The thing is though, no one knows where the dirt road leads until you walk down it. God still had a plan for me even though I chose the harder road.

He kept whispering to me because He wanted to save me. He wanted to get me back on the path of righteousness so we could finish the race together.

1 Corinthians 10:13

"The temptations in your life are no different from what others experience. And God is faithful. He will not allow the temptation to be more than you can stand. When you are tempted, He will show you a way out so that you can endure."

Caylee and Caitlyn

Chapter 4
Rest Areas

I had to come to grips with the truth. I knew my marriage was never going to work. Shaun had gone back out on the road driving trucks and had left me and the girls. We couldn't afford the rent and had nowhere to go. My family had come to their wits end with me. My dad, who had always been the one who helped me no matter what, was deployed–and was tired of helping me. So, for the first time in my life I felt completely and utterly helpless. My mom helped where she could, but my stepdad would never allow us to be a burden to him. Honestly, I can't blame him for that.

I was desperate to get back on my feet, as they say, and make a new life for myself and the girls. I ended up asking the one person I never dreamed I would ask for help–my paternal grandfather. Now granted, he wasn't a mean man at all. He loved his family and would help anyone, especially his children. But our history made it different with me.

When I was eighteen years old, my grandfather tried to apologize to me for the childhood sexual abuse. He rationalized his actions by saying he had a porn addiction. But his confession was made behind a closed door.

His apology was given in almost a whisper so no one would hear him. It was like he regretted what happened but didn't want to admit his guilt to the family. In his own way, I knew he was trying to make amends. I was thankful he was trying, but it made me feel uncomfortable. In his disillusioned confession, he wanted to also confess private issues between him and my grandmother. Maybe it made him feel better to get it off his chest, but it burdened me with knowledge I did not need to know. I was already an outsider in a family where no one dealt with their issues.

There I was broken and messed up, full of the consequences of my mistakes, and abused, both mentally and physically with nowhere to go but to my first abuser. My grandfather was eager to help me. I think it made him happy that I asked for his help.

And I think he wanted a chance to help me.

I assume my grandmother and her daughter discussed my dilemma. I believe it to be my aunt who concluded that it would be best if me and my girls went to stay at the local homeless shelter.

So, with my aunt driving, we headed to that homeless shelter. She took me inside to get registered for an open bed. My aunt was serious when it came to me not being around her parents. That's why she drove me to the shelter herself. As we toured the shelter, I became highly aware of strange men, drug addicted women, and hopeless children. It absolutely terrified me.

I was so afraid that I wouldn't be able to protect my children there. What a thought! As if they had been protected before!

I guess better the devil you know, than the one you don't, right? I remember thinking, "If only my dad were here. If I could just make things right with my dad, I know he would help me." But he wasn't there. I was sitting next to a woman who I felt hated me. I was in such a desperate situation that I asked for help from the one person who did the most damage in my life.

As we sat in the front room of the shelter, waiting for them to find us beds, my aunt's phone rang. I saw her face flush out of frustration. It was my grandfather. He told my aunt to bring me home. He told her he couldn't let me stay there.

To say I was relieved is an understatement. In a bizarre twist, my abuser had now become my savior. He literally rescued me from a nightmare. In an emotional and sincere moment, I said out loud to my aunt that Pop must be willing to help me because he knew what it felt like to make mistakes, need forgiveness, and then help others in return. What I meant in that statement was that I felt my grandfather understood my desperate situation. He knew what it was like to struggle, to make mistakes, and to mess up. He knew what it was like not to have anyone see you through eyes of compassion. He knew I needed help, and without any piousness or hypocrisy, he wanted to help me.

My aunt's response was like a dagger that pierced my soul for decades. She looked me square in the eye, and with a look of hatred said, "My father has never done anything in which he needs to ask forgiveness." I knew she really didn't believe her statement.

I had the secret knowledge of my grandfather's confessions, so I knew he had done things that hurt both my grandmother and his own children. What my aunt wanted to say to me was, "My father has never done anything *to you* in which he needs to ask forgiveness."

It was a gut punch that went all the way down into my soul. At that moment, I knew that she had never believed me. And, that my grandfather had lied to them about everything. I always suspected, but never really knew. It was never again mentioned after my dad confronted them when I was a child. I talked about it at length with my mom, dad, sister, Judy, and all my mom's family. But never a word was mentioned by my dad's family.

She honestly thought I was a liar. Looking back now, I understand why she wanted me to go to the shelter. She thought the abuse was a story that I had made up about my grandfather. She must have been afraid that I would make up other stories about him. She thought she was protecting him from me and my two toddlers. My grandfather knew the truth though. He knew, and deep down, he loved me–and he regretted what he had done.

He wanted to help me, probably as the only way to make restitution for the offense against my innocence. I am forever thankful that he did. It took many more years to be able to forgive him completely, but this action let me know he did care and didn't want me to be harmed. It took me longer to forgive my aunt though.

During the process of writing this book, God helped me release my resentment toward her. It is strange how the bystander is sometimes the one who has the longest affect on the wounded. My grandfather took me and the girls into his home, so it helped me to see him in a different light. But it was still difficult emotionally to have to live with him. I wouldn't let the girls out of my sight. I lived in constant fear that something might happen to them. I hated myself for putting us in this situation. My grandparents truly were great to me during this period of my life and probably saved us from a life of destitution.

I wish I could have told my grandparents how grateful I was for their help before my grandfather lost his memory.

I couldn't freely communicate this at the time. I still needed to work through forgiveness and years of emotional healing. But, after we stayed with them for a while, my grandfather bought this tiny, one-room, red house for me and the girls. It was small. It had a porch area where we watched TV. The kitchen doubled as my bedroom. I managed to squeeze in a twin bed. I put the girls in the actual bedroom. It had bunk beds built into the wall that was adjacent to a very small bathroom.

This little red shack, which most would consider a dump, was my oasis. We had our own place, and I didn't have to pay rent. It was a refuge in the middle of my wilderness. The girls suffered from night terrors. They wouldn't sleep alone, so we ended up all sleeping on the one twin bed in the kitchen. I didn't care. We were together.

We began going to church, and I had started cosmetology school. I was on track to get my life back together. We lived in that shack for months–maybe over a year. I don't remember exactly, but I know it was longer than anyone would have wanted to stay. That Christmas, I didn't have anything for the girls. We received gifts from the Angel Tree donations, and I picked up a few things from the thrift store. Thank God for my parents! They always took care of the girls. They never went without. We would shop thrift stores for several more years, and I became an expert of finding amazing Christmas gifts that made my girls happy.

I had a life changing encounter with God one night in that little red shack. I had always gone to church even when I wasn't living right. I may have missed weeks at a time, but I would find my way to a service somewhere no matter where we lived. There was a deep yearning in my soul for God. He would always pull me toward His heart. I loved Him and desperately needed Him, even when I was spiraling in the wrong direction.

I had heard there was a Shambock tent revival in a neighboring town. I decided to pack the girls up and go to the revival searching for an answer to my situation. I sat through the entire service that lasted hours. Truthfully, it seemed like one big offering call. I remember being so frustrated because I was broke, on welfare, spiritually broken and extremely depressed. What did I have to offer this ministry? I had no money to give, and everything was centered around the offering call.

I was about to get up and walk out of the service when the Holy Spirit prompted me to wait a little longer. After the never-ending offering call, the pastor got up and preached what seemed about a ten to fifteen minute message. Now I may be exaggerating, but that is what I remember.

However, his message hit home. He said if we needed something from God to just ask Him. He instructed us to make a list and to be specific in writing down exactly what we needed from God. Then we were to tell Him. That seemed simple enough. After three hours of sitting in this service, that is what spoke to me. I headed home to the shack, put the girls to bed, and said, *"Okay God! Here it goes. I will make a list."*

I broke down in the ugliest cry you have ever seen. It was a gut wrenching, moving heaven kind of cry to God for help. I let everything spill out of my heart that night. All the disappointment, pain, guilt, shame, anger, resentment, and fear. I gave God everything I had been holding within the depths of my soul. He met me where I was. I made an extremely specific list like the preacher said to do. I vocalized my conclusion that my marriage was over and that I believed no one would ever love me. Looking back, I prayed the kind of prayer that one who doesn't genuinely believe in herself prays. I prayed for a rescuer. Here's my list:

1. A husband who loved me unconditionally and without ties to anyone else–no ex-wives and no ties to any ex-wives

2. A husband who had no kids so he could love my girls one-hundred percent

3. A man who would love my girls as his own

4. And one who made an exact dollar amount

I listed the dollar amount I wanted him to make a year but got nervous. I then lowered it a little to make sure God could handle it.

After I picked myself up off the floor, God shifted something in my spirit. My life changed that night. God came down and met me in a powerful way. He had mercy on me, and I heard Him speak to me, "Let's start rebuilding." Looking at this prayer now, which is one of my most precious God moments, I see the brokenness in my words. I didn't believe in myself, and absolutely couldn't believe that I could rebuild my family. I was searching for someone to save us and love us. God did bring that man to us, but only after he restored me to a healthy spiritual and emotional state.

At the time, I didn't have enough faith in God to pray for financial freedom and security. I never in a million years would have believed that twelve years later, I would be the one making more money than what I had prayed my future husband to make. Although, I didn't believe in myself, God met me in that shack. He not only answered my prayer as I called out my list, but "changed my stars" as well. Father God began to show me that He had unlimited resources.

After that night in the shack, I cried myself to sleep. I didn't have any more energy to expend on living the way I had been living. I was never fully invested in my destructive lifestyle because my heart was always promised to Jesus. I had loved Jesus since before I could remember. That love was always buried in my heart, even when I strayed in living fully for Him. I followed someone whom I chose to put before Jesus. Someone who took over my heart and mind. When you love Jesus, He is always in the picture. He never leaves you. He woos you toward returning to Him. However, you can feel Him grieving over you. I was always conflicted within, and after that night, I knew I had to make a change. I needed to find my way back home.

Within a few months, I ended up calling my dad. He was back from deployment. I humbled myself and apologized for my choices asking him if I could come home. He welcomed me and the girls. He invited us to stay with him and Judy. I am sure it was an awfully hard adjustment for their lifestyle. Judy has always been so gracious. If we inconvenienced her in any way, it never showed. I had graduated cosmetology school and started working at a local hair salon.

We started to rebuild.

Eventually I found a mobile home for sale that was affordable. My dad bought it and let us live there rent free for nine years while I rebuilt the rubble of my life. The first few years were hard. I would have dreams of drugs, or Shaun. Shaun would show up in our lives occasionally, but only for short bursts of time. He then would disappear. I was afraid at night. I would check our windows and doors two or three times a night. We all slept in the same room.

Caylee and Caitlyn adjusted to not seeing their dad. It was extremely hard for them, but also a blessing. Shaun eventually walked away from us completely. He left us entirely empty of resources and moved on. The hurt and pain we suffered because of him and for him broke our hearts. But, after ten years of turmoil, we didn't have anything left to give.

On Caylee's seventh or eighth birthday, Shaun promised to come pick her up and spend time with her. I knew he wouldn't show. I tried to convince Caylee to let me make her a birthday dinner, but she refused. That morning she packed her bag and sat on the porch. Her bag sat next to her while she waited for her dad. She waited for hours. When it started getting dark, she finally came in and cried all night. I had never seen Caylee cry like that before; or come to think of it, ever since.

After that event, she never looked for her dad again. Instead, she focused on the family she had in front of her. It was just me, Caitlyn, and Caylee. The three of us against the world. That mobile home wasn't perfect or new, but it was safe. It's where some of my family's best memories were made.

It was the first stable home my girls ever had and where Sparkles, our pug, came to be a part of our family. It is where I learned to make a turkey for Thanksgiving. Where I stayed up to the wee hours of the morning to study. Where Caitlyn locked her door before going to sleep one night and then slept through the tornado because we couldn't get her to wake up. Where Caylee had her motorized scooter and became a cheerleader. This was our refuge of safety. My sweet Aunt Debbie and Uncle Charlie lived directly across the street from us and watched over us. We were going to be okay!

The next nine years were not easy. In no way did we pray a prayer and wake up the next morning to a world full of bliss. Unfortunately for me, I still had to reap what I had sown over the past decade. I had to make myself wake up in the mornings and go to a job that didn't cover all the bills. I fought depression and loneliness.

During this season, Satan tried convincing me the struggle was harder than the end results were worth. I had been in the apartment business since I was eighteen. So, when I wasn't making enough money to cover our bills using my cosmetology skills, I decided I should go back to what I knew best–managing apartments. It frustrated me seeing families on free housing and free rent programs, receiving free schooling, all because they didn't work. I was tempted many times to quit and just live off the welfare system. I would have received more money from welfare than I was making at the time.

My dad wouldn't have it though. He was a stabilizing force in my life. He pushed me to be successful. He told me that "quitting was not an option." I can't tell you how many times he said that to me. His speech would ring in my ears, "Quitting is not an option! Eventually, all your hard work will pay off! Then you can snub your nose at the naysayers in your life." So, I kept pushing. I kept waking up when I wanted to stay in bed. I kept going to work when it felt useless. I kept going to church when I felt like an outcast. Quitting was not an option for me.

One Sunday morning was particularly difficult as I pulled into the parking lot. Being a single mom is ridiculously hard. Mowing the yard, cleaning the house, being a caretaker and caregiver, working, changing the oil, taking the trash out–all of it can be difficult to handle on your own. It can be overwhelming when you are trying to heal emotionally and help your kids do the same. This particular Sunday was one of those days when nothing seemed to go right.

As we pulled up to the church, I noticed all the families walking into the church building. These were families that I would refer to when I was a teenager as the pretty people. The husbands and wives probably worked out four days a week and drove nice cars. The kids were dressed perfectly with big, bouncing bows in their hair. The boys had on polos and khakis. I saw these seemingly perfect families and then looked at our rag-tag group who could barely get out of bed. I thought to myself, "I will never have what they have. I am not worth anything, and I am too far gone. My kids deserve better than me. I will never amount to anything. No one will ever want me because I don't look like 'that' family and I have nothing to offer."

I broke down in a horrible ugly cry, and just drove off. I couldn't handle going to church that day.

But I didn't stay in that emotionally painful place. I pulled myself together and tried again the next Sunday. And then the next; and then the next. Some days were good, some bad, but I kept trying because "quitting was not an option for me." I knew if I quit that my kids wouldn't have a chance. At this stage in life, I knew I had to make it for their sake. I was going to do my best to give them a normal life. I prayed for God to send me someone who loved me unconditionally–just as I was. I prayed for help in getting a job where I could support my kids.

I started putting applications out, and God did His part. This was the first miracle of many. I received a call from a management company in Dallas looking for a training specialist. I went in for an interview in this fancy high-rise building, with floor to ceiling windows and a glass elevator. I thought my heart would sink into my feet. I jumped into the first restroom I could find, and I cried out to God asking Him to give me favor with the woman interviewing me. That is the day I met Sue Rich.

God used this woman to change my life. She didn't interview me. We just talked for over an hour about random subjects. Sue has a gift of making people feel at home with her and I felt like I was talking to a long-lost friend. We hit it off, and she hired me. She hired me not as an onsite manager, or a leasing agent. She hired me as a corporate training specialist. I now had a job at a corporate office making good money. I couldn't believe it. Sue ended up becoming one of my closest confidants and mentors. She taught me how to use my voice and to be strong. She taught me lessons like, "You can be pitiful, or powerful. Which do you choose?" She taught me that sometimes it was necessary to offend people to keep my boundaries intact.

She taught me that sometimes in life, you need to have what she called a "trash-can-kicking fit" to get things done. She taught me that when I must discipline someone, I also have to love them back up. Within six months of being hired by Sue, I was promoted to a regional supervisor. She had given me the chance, but I took hold of the opportunity, and busted my butt to make it work. I worked harder than I knew possible to make sure I didn't let anyone down again–especially myself.

It is normal on any journey to need to take a break and rest. Some breaks require an intensive care unit like mine did. But some rest stops are there just so you can rest your eyes, refuel, and get some strength back.

I wasn't healed yet, and I needed the help of others to get back on my feet. I needed the help and protection of my family. I needed a safe place to process and heal. When you are in the middle of a battle you don't have the ability to stop and heal. In the time that immediately follows that battle, it is vital that you take time to breathe and recover from the destructive forces that tried to take you out.

It is our responsibility to take hold of those healing seasons. You must move into the harbor of a safe place and allow yourself the ability to grieve, cry, mourn, be angry, and rest. But you can't stay in this place–it is only a rest stop. Some of us take longer because we may have internal bleeding or damage. Just know that you can't stay there forever. God will always strengthen us to start the re-building process.

Matthew 11:28
"Come to me, all you who are weary and burdened, and I will give you rest.

Our safe home

First year back home

Caitlyn, Caylee, and Chase–The Dream Team

Chapter 5

Changing Lanes

This begins the season where I started taking personal inventory and learned about myself. I realized I had been under the thumb of an abusive husband who I put before my own needs. I was also the mother of two amazing children who I also put before my own needs. Truthfully, I had lost myself and didn't know who I was. The realization of that came to me one morning when I was alone making breakfast:

I realized I didn't know how I liked my eggs.

I knew what kind of eggs Shaun had eaten, and I knew what kind of eggs the girls favored–but I didn't know what I liked. I couldn't identify my favorite food, my favorite movie, or my favorite color. For years, I would have told you that my favorite color was blue because that was Shaun's favorite color. It was time to learn about me. I started dating. I dated one man who truly taught me to believe in myself again. He showed me how to eat sushi. I never knew that I loved sushi!

By the way, I like my eggs scrambled with cheese. And my favorite color is pink.

I bought a new outfit for one of these date nights. I was dressed in a fancy black shirt with jeans. I wore a wide red high-waisted belt and finished the look with red high-heeled shoes. I felt like a million bucks. My date took me to this fancy restaurant which was way out of my price range. A valet stepped out and opened the door for me. I was completely out of my element and I loved every minute of it.

We had finished our dinner, and both wanted to freshen up before leaving. I just barely beat my date outside. I saw that he wasn't there and turned around to walk back inside. He appeared right behind me, so we turned back around and walked back outside. Within the few seconds I had stepped out and in and back out again, the valet service had seen me and pulled our car to the door–literally within seconds. I remember thinking, "Wow! They are on it!"

My date saw it differently. He said, "They never do that for me. They saw you and they remembered you. You must have made an impression on the drivers." He was a bit jealous, but also full of pride because of the impression his date had made. I thought to myself, "They saw me? They knew whose car I belonged to? How could they remember that? Wow! They saw me!" I felt seen–and I liked it. This marked the day that I would never again hide in the corner as a wallflower afraid to be seen.

Dating was a way for me to spread my wings, and I had grown in carrying myself with confidence. But I was ready to meet someone who would love me unconditionally. I also needed to get a divorce from Shaun. We had divorced once, and then remarried. At this point, we had been separated for several years. It was time to move on.

I filed for the final divorce and ended it for good. All I wanted was full custody of the girls. Since he never showed up to court, I was ordered full custody and a very minor amount of child support–which I never received. With the divorce behind me, I needed to look toward the future of my little family.

I was tired of being in debt and constantly broke. My life was improving in so many areas, but I still couldn't see a way to support us by myself. I faithfully prayed over my children every night. I prayed that God would make a way for me to provide for them well. At this time, I couldn't even afford a car. My dad had purchased the car I was currently driving. I earnestly prayed that, when the time came, God would provide a way for me to pay for my girl's college, and to be able to buy them cars when they learned to drive.

I wanted to be able to support them the way my parents had supported me. I used to say that if I was stuck on the moon, my dad would find a way to come get me. I wanted to be that kind of parent to my girls. T.D. Jakes preached a sermon saying, “If you want what they have, you have to do what they did!” I have used these words many times throughout my life and career, but learning this lesson started with my dad’s example.

I knew I wanted to be a good parent and have a stable home, with the ability to take care of my girls. I knew that I wanted to be the kind of parent that would fly to the moon to pick up my kids if they needed me. So, I decided to do what he did to get there. I called my dad to discuss my finances.

I was in debt and not even making ends meet. I needed to change the way I handled my finances. I told my dad that I wanted to be more like him and asked if he would take over my checking account. I asked him to give me an allowance until I proved trustworthy to handle it myself.

He took control of my checkbook and all my money. He would pay my bills each week and give me enough for living expenses. I am not going to lie. This was extremely hard for me. Not only was I a grown adult with two children, I also had a corporate job. But now, I had to ask my dad for lunch money.

It was humbling and frustrating, especially when I wanted something, and he didn't feel as though we needed it. During this time, my dad, without me knowing, took the money we had and paid off all my old debt. In the months that we were tight, he would cover any shortfalls. After a few years, my strict budget didn't bother me anymore. It just became my way of life. My dad did this for me for over five years. When it was time for me to take control of my finances again, I was terrified I would mess up everything we had accomplished. I still didn't trust myself, but I had watched my dad's habits over the past five years, and I put them into practice. His habits became my way of life.

With all my debt paid off and my credit clean, I was able to buy a car, and eventually a house. All these years later, those same spending habits come into play. My bills are always paid, and I get extremely anxious if anything is late. I owe this to my dad for being a trustworthy father who taught me hard lessons. But also because I humbled myself and was willing to be teachable.

This is how God works. The Bible tells us in 2 Chronicles 7:14, *"If we humble ourselves and pray, and seek God and turn from our wicked ways, then Father will hear from heaven and will forgive our sin and heal our land."*

I wasn't living the perfect Christian life; but I humbled myself before God, before my earthly father, and I prayed. I had turned from a destructive lifestyle and asked both my Heavenly and earthly father for help. God knew my heart and saw my earnest desire to do what was best in His sight. He used my father to help me. God heard my cry for help and forgave me. Now my life (land) was being healed. God's blessings began to flow and truthfully, they have never stopped.

It was at this point that I started paying my tithes. I was afraid to pay the full 10% so I paid a set amount each pay day. Then I increased that amount a little at a time until I reached 10% of my gross income. My income has increased over sixteen times the amount of what I was making when I first started my journey of financial reformation.

Looking back at that night in the shack when I prayed for a husband to make a certain amount of money, it never dawned on me to pray that I would make that kind of money. I didn't have the faith then to pray that prayer for myself–but God knew where we were headed. He ended up giving me everything I had prayed for, plus some.

He believed in me, even when I didn't believe in myself.

The girls and I had started a new chapter, and we were doing alright. But still, in no way was this chapter easy. In some ways, it was the hardest chapter in my story to date. You see, this is the chapter where I started to make good choices and had to climb out of the proverbial hole that I had dug. This is the season I had to make myself wake up and go to work when all I wanted to do was sleep. This was the season I would pray over my children numerous times a day to protect them from the spiritual forces I allowed in our lives.

I had to break soul ties with Shaun and had to pray generational curses off my children. I had to go to church when I was too tired to get out of bed. I wasn't completely broken anymore, but I wasn't whole. My heart was in the right place, and my love for God was unwavering, but it was still a journey to get back to my first love with God. I wasn't the perfect Christian, but my heart yearned for God. And I prayed constantly.

I tell you these things so that you won't believe the lie that you have to be this picture-perfect person for God to start working in your life. My life was still a mess, although it was getting better. God had a plan for me. He was patient with me. It was a process, and I learned that sometimes the process is more of a marathon instead of a sprint. My journey into stabilization took about ten years.

Some years were harder than others. Some seemed much easier. Looking back, most of the time, I would take two steps forward and one step back, but I kept moving.

Sometimes, I think this was the hardest season yet. Why would I say that? Because when you are the victim, like I was as a child, you don't have a choice. Then, during my marriage, I had choices to make, but I was emotionally controlled and manipulated. Being victimized, or being controlled by life's circumstances, means your life is about one thing–survival. Growing, learning, getting healthy, and making good choices sometimes gets overlooked for the simple fact you are trying to simply survive. Survive what you ask? –Depression, isolation, self-doubt, and a whole host of emotional chains that are placed upon you during the abusive season.

The important thing is to never give up–to keep moving. However, it is the next season that can be the most difficult. You must make the choice to heal, to love others, to love yourself, and to overcome loneliness and abandonment. Your spiritual muscles start to grow and honestly, it is extremely difficult. Especially if you are walking through this while trying to raise kids and pretending your life is normal so they feel normal. It takes every bit of strength you have not to give up!

One hard lesson I learned is that even though I started making right choices, I still had to reap the consequences from my wrong ones. I had to pay my dues, I guess. It would be easy for some to give up during this season because they might feel as though they are doing everything right without seeing the good fruit from their labor. Let me encourage you–don't stop. Keep doing what you are doing. Quitting is not an option. Your good seed will be reaped in the next harvest. If you go backwards, most likely, you will encounter another bad harvest.

My girls are what motivated me the most. I wanted to be a good mom more than anything else. I wanted them to look at me and say, "She loves me! She will be there for me!" We invented our own hand signal. It looked like "I love you" in sign language, except we would leave our middle finger up with the thumb, index, and pinky. It was our own made up “I love you” signal. I think we did this because one of the girls couldn’t make her middle finger stay down when she was small. They used to ask me what the hand signal meant, and I would hold their thumb and say (I) index (love) middle (you) pinky (forever). It was our thing. No matter where we were, or how bad our day seemed, we could give each other that sign. It was a reminder that the three of us had each other.

My Granny was the matriarch in my mom’s family. She was the root system that held the family together. She loved hard and prayed harder. She taught us how to do the same. Her legacy to all of us was a deep love and a knowledge of Jesus Christ. She was the salt and light in our family.

When my mom was little, my Granny had to work numerous jobs to keep the family afloat. My Papa just did not do much to help her, and they had six children. They were poor and had very little at times, but if anyone was in need, my Granny would help them. She would feed them or give them what she had. One time she gave someone who was in need the last of her groceries. My aunt asked her, “Mama what are we going to eat?” My Granny said, “God will provide.” They went to church that day, and when they got home, they had a bill of groceries waiting on them. She had the kind of faith and generosity that changes lives. But like me, she lived in survival mode for her kids’ sake.

My mom tells a story about my Granny that sums it all up. Once, my Granny was walking to the store with her six kids in tow. Her dress was in fashion for the day being back in the 1960’s. It was fitted around the waist and the skirt was sewn with a wide flair. As she was walking with her children, a huge dust storm appeared out of nowhere. She had unknowingly walked her children straight into the storm. Dust and debris whipped around violently. It was difficult to see anything. She had to take cover and wait it out.

My Granny opened the width of her skirt and took all her kids into it. She wrapped them up while she endured the storm. She endured the brunt of the dust, rocks, and debris while doing the best she knew how in sheltering her children.

Storms are certain to come into our lives, but how we react to them is our choice. My Granny chose to protect those she loved. She didn't run from the storm or overreact. She was calm and became a source of security for those in her care. When the storm was over, I am sure she had a few bruises and looked a mess, but she survived, and her children emerged with little damage.

In this season, I found myself in a spiritual storm. I had a choice in how I responded. I could bury my head and sleep, or I could stand up and do the best I knew how to protect my girls. I chose to do my best. I worked hard and I spoke life into my daughters. Again, I wasn't a Pollyanna Christian at this time. I was just trying to make it and put the broken pieces of my life back together. I learned somewhere along the way to use my voice and speak life into my circumstances.

You have the ability to use your voice to speak life or death over yourself.

You can either agree with God's blessing or agree with the devil's accusations.

Our words create our environment. What you speak will come forth in your life.

Even though this rebuilding season was personally one of my most difficult, it also gave birth to some of our best memories. Since we didn't have much, our favorite family night consisted of pizza and a VHS from the movie rental store every payday. We read the entire Twilight book series together. Our house was divided between team Edward and team Jacob. We would stand in line for hours to watch the Twilight marathons at the local movie house when they released a new movie. We bonded together tightly and, later I realized that, looking back on this difficult season, it was one of my favorites. Nothing worth having comes easy, and what doesn't kill you makes you stronger. The life I have with my family now is a life worth having. It was worth every hard day–plus more. I am a stronger person because of the adversity I faced.

I don't regret my life; instead, I cherish it.

Life was better, but I still felt as though I needed someone to be on my side. It was during this time that I ran into an old friend of mine from high school. I think we reunited with each other on Myspace or Facebook. Honestly, I can't remember which. But Jonathan had been one of my very best friends in high school and I was excited to see him. He was quite a goofball–cracking jokes all the time and making people laugh. I could use a laugh. He was a musician and had a gig in Dallas. He invited me to go see him. Seeing him was like a breath of fresh air. He had always been my friend, and I knew I could trust him. I knew he wouldn't purposely hurt me, and he would be there through life's hardest days.

We were inseparable after that and dated for about a year. However, our differences began to surface. He was a musician who was focused on his music. I was career driven. I was determined, or maybe terrified, not to go back to the state of poverty that I had been in before. The days of eating out of the food pantry and having nothing but powdered milk and instant potatoes to feed my kids, still haunted me. Our love for each other and friendship was solid and unmatched, but because we were going in different directions, we decided it best just to remain friends. I had my corporate job but wanted more. I wanted to be the best in my field.

It took about four months after our break-up to figure out that I was pregnant. It was masked because I was experiencing physical issues which required a hysterectomy. I had been putting it off mainly due to being stubborn and refusing to take off work. I truly had no idea that I was pregnant, and when I found out, I was devastated. I literally sat in my car hyperventilating, crying, and overcome with fear. I called my best friend Angela and cried because I just didn't know what to do. I could barely support two kids. How could I support three? I was overwhelmed with the thought of daycare, diapers, formula, and all these expenses again.

What would my family say? How would I tell Jonathan?

I processed all of this for several days. On top of the other thoughts, I was in the middle of building my career. What would this do to my chances of success? All I wanted was to be able to afford to send my girls to college, but how could I ever afford anything again. Then I thought, who would ever want me again? I am an overweight, financially unstable, mother of three. My chances are over for a better life. All these thoughts overpowered me, and I went into a deep depression.

Honestly, I didn't want to write this part of my story. But I feel as though light needs to be shed for someone who might be in a similar situation. I contemplated many ideas during the first few months of pregnancy.

I considered both abortion and adoption.

My sister offered to adopt the baby, but I was afraid of how hard it would be to see someone else raise my child. Abortion seemed like a better option. I know my mind was clouded and I understand how spiritual warfare works. Satan will play on your fears until the lie he is feeding you seems like your only option. Hopelessness and despair ended up plaguing me during the entire pregnancy.

I remember telling Jonathan I was pregnant. It had been quite a while since we had spoken. When I called him, I said, "I have something to tell you, and I need you to be supportive." Then I just blurted it out. He was obviously in shock as we had not been together in months. He said something off-color, and I hung up on him. Then, I immediately called him back. After he had time to process the shock, he told me he was "all in." He had to work through his fear of what people would think since he was a pastor's son, but in the end, he didn't care. He already loved the baby, and I knew this child would always have a loving father.

My older children did not have that promise. This was a legitimate fear of mine. Jonathan's father took me to dinner and told me how important this child was to him. He assured us both how loved my baby would be, and he encouraged me not to carry any fear or shame. Honestly, my depression would become so severe throughout the duration of my pregnancy that I am not sure how Jonathan, or his family, dealt with me. But I am so thankful for their encouragement. They showed my girls and me nothing but love and support.

I came to a place in my mind where I knew I did not believe in abortion. I also knew that I couldn't let someone else raise my child. I finally settled in my heart that I would have this baby. I believe my depression was brought on by the stress of the situation and hormones. I now have so much sympathy for those dealing with depression while pregnant.

I have sense learned that about 20% of pregnant women deal with depression. The depression itself leaves women with regrets. The guilt over feeling like a horrible mom for not instantly loving everything about being pregnant can be difficult to overcome. It is so hard to talk about, but I encourage all women dealing with pregnancy related depression to not give in to shame. Instead, take steps to be the best mom you know how to be by getting emotional help and support for yourself.

My depression was so severe, I was afraid the baby would feel it and be depressed too. I found out that I was expecting another girl and wanted to give her a name that would counteract my depressive state–a name that meant joy. I also wanted to give her Jonathan's first initial. Caitlyn and Caylee had their dad's first initial. His name was Christopher Shaun. I thought it would be fitting if this child did also.

I looked up all the "J" names that meant joy and found several, but the one that stood out was Jovial. I was a huge Bon Jovi fan and decided to shorten Jovial to Jovie. A few months later, Jovie was born.

After meeting her, and bringing her into my life, I would never have wanted it any other way. I fell in love with this child and the depression lifted. I was left with nothing but pure affection for her. The financial issue never materialized. Both my family and Jonathan's family adored this precious girl, and our family grew. All my kids bring something special into my life, but what Jovie has added is joy. I look at her and she makes me laugh. When she cuddles with me, it makes my heart skip. She says off the wall random jokes that are so goofy they are funny. God used this little girl to bring tremendous joy out of deep depression.

Anyone thinking of abortion, or giving up, please reconsider. I promise you Satan is a liar and God doesn't create anyone that isn't meant to bring Him glory.

Jovie was meant to be a part of this family. She has a purpose to fulfill in God's Kingdom. My life would be less without her in it. Jonathan and I built a beautiful friendship and co-parent better than anyone I have met. He is still my best friend, and all of us trust him. He is always there for me and each one of my girls when we need him. He is an amazing father who showers Jovie with love and affection. I could not ask for a better Pops, Grammy, or Daddy for Jovie. What seemed so bad all turned out so good. It just wasn't wrapped in the pretty package we expected.

During this season of my life, I was not living perfectly, but I was at least walking down the road that leads to righteousness. I still sinned and made mistakes, but God continued to bless me. He knew where I was headed and was proud of me for leaving the tough places I had been.

Just like our earthly children, we root for them on the journey of life. We choose to bless them even when they are less than perfect because we can see where they are headed and what they are trying to achieve.

God knew I had to walk a long road to get to restoration. That road was not always pretty, nor easy. But, He has grace for us during these seasons. He knows our hearts, our desires, and our struggles. He sees the sleepless nights where we toss and turn desiring a better life, the lonely nights we cry ourselves to sleep, and the mornings we wake up and dress ourselves for battle to move forward one inch at a time. He sees us and says, "I am proud of you."

Mandy Owen

Daniel 9:9

"But the Lord our God is merciful and forgiving, even though we have rebelled against Him."

Jovie Rosemarie

Chapter 6
Yielding to Rewards

When Caitlyn was in sixth grade, she had to do a project for school. Her assignment was to create a family crest. She didn't tell me about this project. That was the norm for us.

I worked all the time and couldn't help the girls with their homework the way I would have liked. But they were both bright girls, and responsible when working on their own. Caitlyn finished her project and turned it in, but afterwards she presented it to me.

Her project was a good example of a message I heard Pastor Robert Morris teach concerning blessings and rewards. He recalled a story about his daughter. She saw him blessing others in private and wanted to be like him. He talked about how much that touched his heart. It was more than a blessing; it was a reward–a badge of honor he could wear on his heart. When I heard him speak about God rewarding our efforts of doing the right thing repeatedly, it touched me. He said that the blessing is not always something tangible, but sometimes it is a deeply rooted reward within your soul. That is what Caitlyn's family crest was for me. It was more valuable and precious than any tangible gift.

She had to draw a family crest with four boxes: one for your mom, one for dad, one for the future and then one for the present. She drew two crests because she couldn't decide which one to turn in. In my box she had Rosie the Riveter. In her dad's box she had a bottle of alcohol. In her present box she had a happy family. And, in her future box she drew an apple symbolizing a teacher.

Her second crest was a little different. In my box was a heart, and in her dad's box she drew a devil with a dollar sign. Her present box still had a cross representing Jesus, and in her future, she drew the coast guard symbol.

When I looked at these drawings, it was the first time I realized that my kids were not immune to the effects of all that had happened. They felt all the struggles I dealt with throughout the years, but they never spoke of it. Maybe they simply didn't know how to vocalize it. There I stood with my sixth-grade daughter explaining to me what her family crest meant to her.

It filled me with joy and broke my heart at the same time.

She said my box with Rosie the Riveter was because I never gave up and fought for our family. She knew no matter what, our motto would be "we can do it." My box with the heart was because she loved me, and she knew I loved her. I was overjoyed and received a "deeply rooted reward" through her that day. She loved me and saw me as someone in her life that would never give up. At that moment, knowing she knew my heart made all the pain we went through worth it.

What broke my heart was how she felt about her dad. I never wanted the girls to hate their dad. I knew it would hurt them more than him. I tried to explain that he loved them, but he had too many problems to be a normal healthy father. I used to try to protect them from the pain of believing they were unloved. At some point though, actions speak louder than words. Their dad's actions toward them affected their thoughts about him.

Caitlyn told me she drew alcohol in his boxes because he was an alcoholic, and all he cared about was his next drink. The devil with the dollar sign was because we only heard from him when he needed money. At that moment, I desperately wanted to change her opinion of him and fix all the pain that our past had caused her, but I couldn't. I had to accept her views and let her feel her pain.

This was the hardest part of my journey watching my girls feel unloved when in fact they were loved more than life itself. Their love, and the love I had for them, was what God used to save me all those years ago. Had I not had to make choices based out of my deep love for my girls, I may never have changed my life. Some days the only reason I got out of bed was for them. However, that day receiving Caitlyn's gift caused joy to overshadow my sadness, and my heart grew bigger. I was overcome with love, and it was given to me by God, and Caitlyn.

Caitlyn's life had not been easy as a child. She had to grow up without her father–which I know hurt her.

Looking at this crest, I knew that I could have made the same choices he did. My box might not have been Rosie the Riveter, or a heart. I feel that if I had not made the choices to change my life when I did, my boxes on that crest would have been worse than her father's.

A mother's love for her children is a powerful tool in God's hands. Fathers are vital as well, but a mother's love is something special. Had I not changed the course of my life when I did, Caitlyn could have drawn dark, angry symbols of hurt in my box. I certainly had not been a perfect mom. I made more mistakes than I ever dreamed I could make. My girls suffered from those mistakes which haunted me for years, but in this instance my daughter let me know, *"Mom, I see you as Rosie the Riveter. Someone who has the attitude of 'We can do it!' You are strong and a fighter. I see you as love because I know you love me."*

Whoa! Now that is a "deeply rooted reward" for my soul. It is never too late to change your path. Quitting is not an option. Little people are watching you, and they will know they are loved by your actions.

There have been so many times I felt that my girls deserved much better than me. If they had been born into one of the "pretty church families," their life would have been easier. They would not have suffered. I felt this way especially when we endured hardships. I would feel guilty believing that everything was my fault. If I had only done things better, my daughters would not be suffering.

Caylee is the one who helped me overcome this. She has come to me on a few different occasions and said, "Mom, I don't know where we would be without you." Now for those who know Caylee, she is a creature of few words and is not one to give a compliment without reason. When she does speak, it is with deep thought and usually pierces the soul of the hearer. So, when she reminds me of this, I know she genuinely feels it in her heart. I don't deserve these "deeply rooted soul rewards." I can certainly say they were not earned through being perfect. They are given freely from Caylee because of fearless love. Even though I may have caused more damage than good in their lives at times, she knows I love her without question. She knows that I never gave up on us. The more I worked on myself, the more I became the mom they needed and deserved.

In the ten years since my breakdown in East Texas and calling my dad to help me, I had thrown myself into not going backwards. Some days, I just barely kept my head above water. Some days, I would sink but float back up. Some days, I seemed to be flying high above the water.

I am not going to lie. My journey was extremely hard, but God had a plan from day one. I felt like I had been in survival mode for the past ten years. I had picked myself up by my bootstraps, tucked my kids under my arms, put my head down in a battle stance, and said, "Okay world, here I come! You're not going to stop us anymore!"

I had thrown myself into my job, climbing the corporate ladder to prove to myself that I wasn't a loser. I prayed for favor at every job, position, property, and relationship that came my way. I never turned any opportunity down. Every door God opened; I ran through–sometimes having no clue what I was doing.

Somehow God had it all under control. He taught me what I needed to know.

Luckily for me, it didn't take being a rocket scientist or having a scholar's degree to do well in property management. It took people skills, team building, mentorship, problem solving, budget control, and management of assets. I like to tease people and tell them that one of God's gifts to me was an extra dose of common sense; and the ability to look at a situation and figure out the needed solution.

Those two God-given gifts set me up for extreme favor in the property management industry. Looking back, I can see God's hand in placing me onto difficult properties. They were like a boot camp, training me on how to handle tough situations and testing me to make sure I was ready for the next opportunity. Over this ten-year period, my salary increased each year–and in some cases, doubled. I began supervising a property in Waxahachie, Texas. We had a leasing agent named Elaine who ended up being one of my dearest friends. *And she kept talking to me about her brother.*

Elaine was very persistent. Every time I saw her, she told me that I needed to meet her brother. I was single with three kids and, at this point, just didn't feel that marriage or a long-term relationship was in the cards for me. After Jovie was born, I had decided to focus on my career and my children. Anymore dating for me would need to take place after the girls were out of high school. I didn't want men in and out of their lives. Honestly, most of the men I saw on the dating apps just seemed creepy.

But Elaine would not quit. She is like a dog on a bone until she accomplishes her goal. So, to get her to leave me alone, I told her she could give her brother my Facebook information. He could message me if he liked. I figured he would see me on Facebook and not be interested. Or I could just blow him off and be done with it.

Needless to say, her brother was just as persistent as she. He messaged me on Facebook and pushed me to give him my number. He started calling me and we would talk for hours. Then he pushed me to go on a date.

Honestly, I didn't want to go.

I felt as though it would never work. I had three kids with no real financial security and a ton of baggage. Who would want us? I was concerned that he might be controlling, abusive, and manipulative. I mean something had to be wrong with him, and what if he was abusive to my children? I tried so hard to not go on this date, but Marc was not only persistent, he was patient.

I would not allow him to know where I lived. I told him I would meet him at his house. Then we could drive to dinner together. When I got in his truck, he had a bouquet of flowers and the newest Bon Jovi CD sitting in the seat. I was not used to anyone giving me gifts. It took my breath away. He didn't even know me, and yet was so nice to me. We went to dinner and to the drive-in. "It was a great date." I went home and thought to myself, "He is so nice. This will never work. It's too good to be true. He must be hiding something."

I started looking for every reason for it not to work. Our second date was a little disastrous. Jovie was only two years old and had a very low immune system. She could get extremely sick in the matter of hours. Marc had invited me to a Texas Rangers baseball game. I didn't want to go because, deep-down I was afraid of where this thing was leading.

As we walked into the stadium my mom called me and told me that something was very wrong with Jovie, and we needed to take her to the hospital. I told Marc I had to leave. He offered to take me to the hospital, but I wasn't ready for him to meet my family. I politely declined and asked him to take me to my car.

I thought this would be it. He would get annoyed for losing so much money on the game and wasting the day he would just call it off. That is not what happened.

Instead, the next day, he called me and said I owed him another date. I felt deep down that I did owe it to him for wasting so much of his time and energy, but I still felt that he needed someone other than me. My focus was on raising my girls. The drama that comes with a house full of females can be overwhelming.

I had decided I would go on the third date and then break it off. Much to my surprise though, the third date was amazing. He cooked me dinner and had flowers waiting for me. He talked to me for hours. He wanted to know all about me and the girls.

That third date was the one that did it for me. I knew after that night that I wanted to give this thing we had going a try. I still had thick walls of protection surrounding my heart. Marc was so patient with me that first year. I was a terrible girlfriend. My walls were impenetrable. Every ounce of love he gave me, bounced off like rubber. I didn't want to get hurt. I was afraid that if I let this man into my world, he would just hurt me. So, I pushed him away constantly, until finally something happened. We got into an argument, and I just walked out. I left, and he let me leave.

Bon Jovi has a song called *Superman Tonight.* The chorus goes: *Who's gonna save you when the stars fall from your sky? And who's gonna pull you in when the tide gets too high? Who's gonna hold you when you turn out the lights? I won't lie. I wish that I could be your superman tonight. If someone sent you an Angel to save you, would you tell him to turn him away? That your heart don't break? That your lips don't kiss? That your life is just a lie? That heaven don't exist? Who's gonna save you when the stars fall from your sky? Who's gonna pull you in when the tide gets too high? Who's gonna hold you when you turn out the lights? I won't lie. I wish I could be your superman tonight?*

Who's gonna fix you the next time you break down? Stranded alone by the side of the road. It's your baggage that's dragging you down. Don't look back. Let it go.

After we broke up, this song rang in my head. I hope you don't misunderstand me. Marc was not my savior. I have only one Savior, One God, and One true love of my life–Jesus Christ. He is the only one who can truly rescue me, fix me, restore me, and make me whole. However, this song rang true in my heart.

I had pushed a man away from me that I knew God had sent. He was someone who God would use to save me when the stars around me started to fall. And someone God would use to pull me in tight when the tide of life got too high. He was someone to hold me at night when the world felt out of control. No one else was going to show up and fix me. I had to give it to God, and let my baggage go.

I knew it was my own baggage weighing me down.

God can speak to us through anything. He used Bon Jovi to teach me a life lesson about risk–about letting someone in who just might be placed there by God Himself. Unfortunately, I figured this out after I walked out on Marc. Now, Marc would not take my calls. I was too proud to make a huge effort and he was moving on. I just decided to let it go.

It's important for people who have been extremely damaged by past relationships to listen to their "safe people." I didn't trust myself, but my "safe people"–my mom, sister, dad, Judy, and aunts and uncles–all loved Marc. They felt he would be perfect for me. Had I listened to them and not pushed him away, we would not have split up those three months. I used to call my sister and tell her, *"This is too good to be true. He is too nice. It won't last. Maybe he is really a serial killer.."* She would say,

"Those things might end up being true, but you deserve a chance at happiness."

She believed that he was a good fit for me. You shouldn't entrust yourself to everyone in your sphere of influence, but you should have an inner circle who will be honest with you, no matter what. You need "safe people" that only have your best interest at heart. Those are the people you go to when the voices in your head get confusing. Sometimes, these people don't tell you what you want to hear but heed their warnings and insights. It might save you years of heartache.

Two of my "safe people," my Uncle, Robert Maston, and my sister, Christy Maston (now McGuyer), decided to intervene in the breakup. They felt Marc and I were meant to be together, and since we were not fixing things, they took it into their own hands to do so. They invited Marc to dinner, and he accepted. I am not sure what they talked about that night, but whatever it was, it must have moved Marc.

Then, they decided to ambush me. They invited me over to my sister's for game night. When I walked in, Marc was sitting at the table. I felt completely bamboozled. I can't remember anything we talked about that night. I was so taken back and annoyed, but deep-down, happy to see him at the same time. We left, and I prayed, "God, what just happened?" On Marc's way home, he asked God for a sign. He asked if I was the person he was supposed to be with. When he turned on his radio, Bon Jovi was singing Livin' on a Prayer: *"We've got to hold onto what we've got. It doesn't make a difference if we make it or not. We've got each other, and that's a lot for love. We'll give it a shot."*

He knew immediately that God was speaking to him about us. It's funny how God used Bon Jovi to speak to both of us. But hey, God uses anything when we have listening ears. He texted me that night and asked me to go to dinner that weekend. We had a hard conversation over dinner, but we patched things up. We have been together ever since.

This is the cool part! A few weeks later, as I was driving, God reminded me of that night in the red shack ten-years earlier when we had nothing–when I was broken into a thousand pieces. He reminded me of my desperate prayer and the list I had written of what I needed in a husband:

1. I had prayed for a husband who would love my children as his own

2. A husband who didn't have any biological children so he would love mine

3. A husband who had never been married or had no ties to an ex-wife

4. A husband who would love me and made a specific salary

It had been ten years since I prayed that desperate prayer. God basically slapped me in the face with the revelation that Marc was all of these! How did I not see this before? Marc had been married for twelve-years but had no biological children from that relationship. His wife had passed away and he had no ties from that relationship. He went through a short six-month rebound marriage to whom he had no ties to anymore. He had no children of his own, and he not only wanted love in his life, but he also had a lot of love to give. He also made the exact amount of money I had asked. I tease Marc sometimes saying had my faith been stronger, he would be in a higher income bracket.

I knew then that God answered my prayer ten-years ago. He answered it that very night, but Jesus needed to get me to a healthy place to receive the answer. God was also working on Marc to get him to a place where he was the man we needed. The prayer was answered immediately, but it took ten-years to birth. It also amazes me how little faith I had when I prayed this prayer. I was desperately crying out to God, and He heard me. I didn't believe in myself at all and felt I needed a husband to rescue me.

What I didn't see was the work God was going to do in me. He built me into a powerful woman of faith, AND a career woman!

"Wow God! Really? Your ways are not my ways, and your thoughts are not my thoughts. You amaze me daily!"

God sent Marc to me because He knew what was needed in bringing a sense of stability to me and the girls. Marc also brought strength, kindness, peace, generosity, and love into our home in a way we had never experienced from a man.

It was not easy for him to come into a home with four girls. Three of us still carried extreme pain from our father/husband relationships– and none of us had a clue how to treat a father or husband. Marc also had a lot of growing to do to learn how to be who we needed. He had his own baggage he needed to work through to love on a deeply intimate level.

But Marc was patient and kind. He didn't try to take control or demand his way. He allowed us to work on building trust in our home. God did show me that I could trust him and eventually, I was willing to give him the reins. He had to grow into the man we needed, and we had to grow into a place of acceptance.

Blended families are not easy because of the emotions of everyone involved. But, when you are patient and put in the work, it is so worth it. Marc and I are meant to be together, and we complement each other in a special way. He is strong where I am weak. I am strong where he is weak. He loves God and is one of the humblest men I have ever met. I am so blessed to have him in my life. He cares for me and our family in such a beautiful way. We were both broken, but God brought restoration to us and gave us each other.

Mathew 7:7-8
"Keep on asking, and you will receive what you ask for. Keep on seeking, and you will find. Keep on knocking, and the door will be opened to you. For everyone who asks, receives. Everyone who seeks, finds. And to everyone who knocks, the door will be opened."

Caitlyn's family crests

Me and Marc at the Texas Ranger's game

Chapter 7
Motion

Marc and I, together, formed a team that complimented each other; and we were able to serve others. I began to hear God clearly. My spiritual ears were opened. I had been deeply returning to God over the past several years and doing my best to live in accordance with His word. My feet were firmly planted on the road of righteousness, but certainly, I was no stranger to the spiritual process.

Sometime after meeting Marc, I felt God tugging at my heart to visit House of Praise–the Linker's church. The tug would not leave me alone. I knew I had to go. Marc, being raised in the Church of Christ, was leery of charismatic churches, but he visited because of me and the girls. I knew God sent Marc to us, but I also knew if I were to marry him, we would need to be on the same page when it came to spiritual matters.

I had prayed about it and given it to God because I knew, if Jesus brought Marc to me, He had a plan. We visited House of Praise and knew instantly we were supposed to be there. Marc and I were married and that began a season of spiritual refinement. House of Praise became a safe harbor for us. We had friends. God used this time to build us up in the Spirit; to hear Him and live in obedience. Pastors Ben and Mel are excellent teachers. The seven-year season in which we attended HOP taught Marc things he had never known and gave me a chance to stretch my spiritual muscles again.

I remember one Sunday morning, Pastor Ben shared that he desired the purpose for which God created him to come to pass *in its fullest capacity*. I had never prayed that prayer before. It was like a lightbulb went off in my spirit. I started praying continually that I would not miss my purpose and that it would be fulfilled to its fullest capacity. After I saturated my thinking and prayer life with this thought, God started shifting my desires beyond my career and family, and into something bigger. I started thinking about the community, about the state, about the country, and about the nations. God started planting more of his dream inside of me.

I was reminded of a prophet who visited HOP shortly after we started attending. I had prayed a prayer that evening before going to hear him speak. I asked God if He remembered the prayers I had prayed when I was a nineteen-year-old in the Master's Commission. I reminded Him of those prayers–before all my bad choices; the prayers I desperately prayed hoping for an answer about my calling. The prayers I prayed asking about my purpose. The prayers I prayed after Pastor Scott's message, and I heard nothing but crickets. The prayers I prayed where I felt as though I received no answer which caused a rift in my spirit. The ones that caused me deep-down to get angry at God for not wanting to use me the way He seemingly used everyone else.

I humbled myself before God knowing He was real and wanting to accept whatever He had for me. I asked Him if He remembered those prayers, and if He could answer them now. Crying to Him I asked, *"Is there a purpose for my life and what do you want from me?"*

That night, as the prophet preached, he called me out. We had never met, but he said that there was someone in the section where I sat named Marie (my name is Mandy Marie and my family often calls me Marie). It felt as though Father was using intimate knowledge of my middle name to lovingly call me forward. *He said that God heard me all those years ago when I was a teenager, and He had my answer.*

He said a few other things that I can't remember, but I did know that I had just prayed and asked God if he remembered my prayers. At that moment, I knew God heard me all those years ago and, He heard me today. I also knew that my purpose was coming into alignment with God's timing, and that He was about to show me what I needed to do. He didn't ignore me all those years ago. He knew the plan. He had a purpose. He wanted me and designed me to be used by Him. I just wasn't ready when I was nineteen years old. Had He told me what my future had in store then, I would have been angry or hurt. Instead, He waited until my heart was ready, and I knew it was Him.

God began using both Marc and me in ministry to help, serve, lead, and bless people in need. We helped the church or community with whatever came across our path. At the same time, I was also promoted in my career to Vice President of Operations, specializing in providing affordable housing to low-income families.

Wow! How the tables had turned from being homeless to providing homes to those in need. I now help single moms, elderly people, homeless, and the abused find a safe place to sleep at night.

My aunt's prophecy of "Mighty, Mighty, Mandy Mo" really starts here. This is where my story begins, and this is where I find my voice. This is the season where I became a spiritual warrior–mighty and fierce. I have had the opportunity to share my story on several occasions. Each time God's goodness overwhelms me, but where I see the most action is in my prayer room. I see spiritual walls come down as I declare victory over my family. I feel the anointing of my Granny as I learn to pray the way she prayed. Marc and I have been prophesied over, that we are stronger together–which is true. We complement each other beautifully, and as we continue to touch the people in our lives, we will do it together in love.

As a teenager, I read the Janette Oke book "Love Comes Softly." Sometimes love comes like a hurricane and sometimes love comes softly. Our love came softly. Truly we have grown into our love for each other. As our roots grow deeper, our love grows deeper. I can't wait to see how God uses us in the future. Our story is just beginning, and God knows how to use all the experiences of the past twenty years in the process.

I have learned so many lessons from mistakes, experiences, mentors, pastors, family, and friends. Through it all, I had a heart to hear God's voice. Then later, I had ears to hear. I wasn't perfect and I made plenty of mistakes, but I have always been a mover by nature. I didn't sit still, and I wasn't afraid to step out. Some of those steps hurt me tremendously. But most of them lead to the next step, then the next, which led to a new path–a new road which led to growth.

As I read the Bible, I see it is full of characters that were also movers by nature. The ones who made big moves are the ones we remember. Most of them have been tainted by sin and their mistakes are not hidden, but God honored them and used them.

I love the story of Tamar. She was dealt a bad hand and anyone reading her story can't argue that what she did to claim her rightful spot within Judah's family was wrong. However, what I see when I read her story is a woman who was strong. A woman who could have sat at her parents' house as a widow and died, but instead, chose to fight back. She decided to claim her spot in her inheritance or die trying. She made a move, whether it was right or wrong.

God saw her heart.

She became the mother of Perez who is listed in the genealogy of Christ. Now God could have chosen anyone to continue His lineage, but He chose Tamar. *Why?*

I also love the story of Rahab the prostitute who is also listed in the genealogy of Christ. She also chose to make her move. No one will argue that prostitution was wrong, but we don't know her circumstances, or her history. Was she in survival mode trying to support herself and her family? What we do know is that when it was time for her to trust God and make her move, she did.

These women are part of Jesus's people–his family. Jesus could have placed himself in a snow-white family full of perfection, but He chose a family full of "dirt road" stories. *Why? Maybe, to reach "dirt road" humanity–those just like you and me.*

What about Joseph? He was dealt a bad hand in life as well. He was sold into slavery meaning, he was homeless, hungry, mistreated, and humiliated daily. Was this God's plan for him? Would Joseph have become the leader he is known for if he never experienced hunger? Would he have had the compassion he displayed if he never experienced abuse? Would he have had the wisdom he gained if he was not put into situations that forced him to rely on God for survival?

Joseph was a mover by nature. He chose radical obedience each time the door opened. He faced every hardship ready to fully serve and allowed God to move in his life. If he had stopped and said, "No more. I give up!" he would have lost everything God was building through his life.

The list could go on and on. We could include David, Moses, and Ruth. I am no different, and neither are you.

The question is, "Do we choose to move or stop dead in our tracks?" For me quitting was not an option! And, I have learned that when God says, "Move!" I move.

Looking back on my life, Newton's Laws of Motion where clearly in place. Newton's 1st Law of Motion states that *every object in a state of uniform motion will remain in that state of motion unless an external force act upon it.* Meaning, you will stay on the path you are on unless another force causes you to change directions.

For me (as a child) there was a force that came against my will when abuse entered my life. It changed my path. Then, in my early twenties, it was my choice to rebel against God and choose a life that led toward destruction. In my adult life, it was the bang that I did not know how to escape (even though I had countless whispers) that hit my life and caused catastrophic damage to me and my girls. This bang caused damage, but also was the force that led to Newton's Second Law being realized.

Newton's Second Law of Motion states *Force=mass x acceleration.* Simply put, the force of an object is determined by the acceleration of an object multiplied by its size (mass).

For me I needed to turn my life around and it was going to be a process. I was going full force in one direction, and my life was a huge mass of problems. To stop full force and turn around without any damage would have been unrealistic. My dear friend Kristene O'Dell gave me an encouraging word about this very thing. She said she saw the Holy Spirit as the net force, and the mass is all that has been accumulated in the Spirit that Father is ready to use for His glory.

It would take a powerful force (the Holy Spirit) to turn me the other direction. Then, I needed the mass (what was accumulated in the Spirit) multiplied by acceleration (my movement) to propel me back on track. Once I regained my footing, I would have to gain momentum again.

Newton's Third Law of Motion states that *for each action there is an equal and opposite reaction.* This is the easiest of Newton's laws to understand and the one that's most familiar. It means that for each action we make, an opposite reaction occurs. I could see this law in action in my life all throughout my rebuilding stage. Looking back over all the lessons I learned, and continue to learn, each has an action and reaction.

When I repented and turned away from my sinful lifestyle, I asked God to forgive me. The reaction was receiving forgiveness and freedom from all my baggage. My past sins were no more. God covered them with His blood and broke their power over me.

When Sue told me to choose to be pitiful or powerful, I chose to stop feeling sorry for myself. The reaction was an abundant and successful mindset.

When my family encouraged me to give Marc a chance, I chose to let my walls down. The reaction was a loving relationship that healed my heart.

When I heard Oprah say that forgiveness occurs when we give up the hope that the past could have been any different–that spoke to me. I had tried often to forgive those who hurt me, but couldn't. When I chose to accept the fact that the past was what it was, and it couldn't be any different, I began to forgive. I could give up my wishful longing for a past that was non-existent and accept the life I had lived.

Forgiveness came in stages for me. I took it one step at a time, and it would take many. I made many trips to the altar praying about and releasing unforgiveness, only to pick it up again later. Later in life, when I was healthier, I was able to truly forgive. I was able to love the people who had hurt me with the love of Christ. The reaction from that choice of forgiveness was complete freedom from the oppression of those hurtful situations.

I was also taught that obedience to the word of God meant tithing. I started by tithing a small portion of my income until I was ready to increase the amount. My faith was built, and I was able to tithe the full ten percent. Even though I wasn't living completely righteously, God honored His principles set in place. When I started tithing, my finances started to change. God used people like my dad to teach me wisdom, and job opportunities came out of nowhere. I was given favor at work, and promotions started coming my way. The more I tithed, the more I was blessed.

Please do not misunderstand my motives for tithing. I wasn't looking for material blessings, I simply wanted to be obedient. However, God blessed me beyond measure.

When I chose to set boundaries around my family and focus on my children, the reactive motion set in place was a sense of safety and the ability to grow as a family. I can remember one tearful conversation with Pastor Scott back in high school. I was upset over not having any friends. I felt alone. I wanted him to pray over me and agree with me that all those other kids were truly awful. Instead, he just patted me on the back and said, "Well, to have friends, you must be a friend," and walked off.

I chewed on that statement well into my late twenties. I realized what he meant years later as I began rebuilding my life. I had to let my walls down and be a friend to people. When I stopped making everything about me and being afraid of being hurt, I started being friendly to people. The reaction set in motion was their friendship toward me. Learning to be a friend brought me a great amount of respect, love, and acceptance.

When I chose to give up food or pleasures in order to set aside time to fast; the reaction was a closeness to God and an intimate relationship with Him. I saw doors open and prayers answered.

When I chose to wake up early in the morning to read my Bible and pray before work, the reaction was an understanding of the heart of God. He moved from being my King and Father, to being my Love and my Friend.

This list could go on and on, but what I want you to see is that Jesus is the way to freedom–whatever your past holds. *Don't let your past dictate your future. Cry out to*

God and start your journey today! You will find that each action you take to turn toward God, will have an equal reaction that brings healing from your pain. Jesus can change the course of your life. He can change your stars just like He did mine.

If you have started your journey, but feel like giving up, "Don't!" Just like the advice my dad gave me, *"Quitting is not an option."* Keep going; keep fighting; and keep praying. You don't have to be perfect, just keep moving.

God will bring your breakthrough, and He will change your circumstances. If I had quit, all my forward motion would have never been realized. If I would have given in when it got hard to breathe each day, I would not know the joy of living this miraculous life I have been given.

I used to be fearful of the blessings that God gave me. I felt like I didn't deserve them, and that something would happen to take it all away. I don't have those fears anymore. Now, I look at my life and I think what does He have for me next?

I look at Caitlyn, Caylee, and Jovie and I am overcome with joy and love as I watch them grow. I watch Chase, and his son, my precious grand-nephew Jude, and I am excited for their future. I look at my mom, dad, and Judy, and am so grateful for my parents. I am thankful for a sister who does life with me.

I am thankful for Marc who loves me, as difficult as I am to love at times. He is a man of God who I can walk through life with, whether good or bad, as we help as many people as we can help along the way.

Most of all I am thankful for a forgiving God who uses those who were once broken to heal the weak–so that they too become strong. I am thankful for my precious Jesus whose love for me is deeper than I can fathom–a love that I never knew was for me. I am blessed beyond measure.

I have been on many roads in my life.
All with unique twists and turns.

I have been on highways of spiritual growth.

I have been on expressways of raising children.

I have been on turnpikes of family ups and downs.

I have been on avenues of education.

I have been on roads of healing.

I have been on boulevards of a great career.

But this–this was my dirt road story.

And, my dirt road led to Jesus Christ.

Johns 3:16
"For this is how God loved the world: He gave his one and only Son, so that everyone who believes in him will not perish but have eternal life. God sent his Son into the world not to judge the world, but to save the world through Him."

This is what a
REALLY COOL
GRANDPA
looks like

Jesus truly does know how to turn sorrow into joy!

About the Author

Mandy is a wife and mother to three amazing girls. She began a career in property management as a leasing consultant in 1995 for a national property management company. Throughout her career, she has grown to become a leader in affordable and conventional housing, specializing in distressed assets. She has also served in many different roles within church leadership as well as serving as a commissioner on her local City Planning and Zoning board.

Marc, Mandy, and the girls attend Freedom Fellowship International–a church where people are encouraged to appropriate the freedom that Jesus desires to give to its fullest measure. You may find Freedom on the web at https://www.freedomonline.com

An online campus is available for those not in the North Texas area.

Made in the USA
Middletown, DE
26 May 2023

30809377R00106